TEAM ENERGIZERS
Fifty Practical Team Activities

Kristin J. Arnold

QPC Press
Fairfax, Virginia

TEAM ENERGIZERS
Fifty Practical Team Activities

Kristin J. Arnold
Copyright © 2003
All rights reserved

Printed in the United States of America
First printing 2003

Arnold, Kristin J.
    Team energizers : fifty practical team activities /
Kristin J. Arnold. – 1st ed.
    p. cm – (The extraordinary team series ; 3)
    Includes bibliographical references and index.
    LCCN: 2002090661
    ISBN: 09676313-2-7

    1. Teams in the workplace. 2. Group games.
I. Title. II. Series.

HD66.A763 2002   658.4'036
                           QBI02-200267

Published by: QPC Press
11304 Megan Drive
Fairfax, Virginia 22030
800.589.4733
www.qpcteam.com

Cover Design: Marnie Deacon Kenney
Interior Illustrations: Shannon Parish

Disclaimer

This book is designed to provide basic information about team activities. It is not the purpose of this book to reprint all the information that is otherwise available on the vast subject of team activities, but to complement, amplify and supplement other professional journals and books. You are urged to read other available references, learn as much as possible about team activities and tailor the information to your individual, team and organizational needs.

The author and QPC Press shall have neither liability nor responsibility to any person or entity with respect to any loss or damage caused, or alleged to be caused, directly or indirectly by the information contained in this book.

If you do not wish to be bound by the above, you may return this book to the publisher for a full refund.

Table of Contents

Foreword   v
Acknowledgements   vi
Preface   vii

1. Aardvark and Antelope   1
2. Active Listening   3
3. Affinity Nametag   5
4. Assigning Priority: Make It All Fit   7
5. Brainstorming Variations   9
6. Break Out Groups   11
7. Build an Agenda   13
8. Building an Extraordinary Team   15
9. Chain Story   17
10. Change!   19
11. Check In & Check Out   21
12. Cliché Bingo   22
13. Decisions, Decisions   25
14. The Deck of Cards   27
15. Face the Facts   31
16. Follow the Process   33
17. Gordian Knot   35
18. The Hats We Wear   37
19. H-O-M-E-S Is Where the Heart Is   39
20. The Huddle   41
21. Johari Window   43
22. Juggling Priorities   45
23. Just Plane Parts   47
24. Map It!   49
25. Odyssey of the Mind   51
26. QTIP   53
27. Quick Vote   55
28. Rainbow Connections   57
29. Read All About It!   59
30. Red Dot, Blue Dot   61
31. Save Everybody!   63
32. Soda Can Carry   65
33. The Sound of Music   67
34. Streamline the Process   69
35. Stretch Goals   73
36. Tea Time   75
37. Team Process Puzzle   77
38. Team Openers   81
39. Test for Consensus: A Straw Poll   83
40. Tinker Toys®   85
41. To Build a Bridge   87

42. To Build a Tower   89
43. To Build a Tower, Version Two   91
44. Tug of War   93
45. Walking Our Talk   95
46. The Web We Weave   97
47. When Shall We Meet Again?   99
48. Where Are We Going?   101
49. Win or Lose?   103
50. You're the Expert!   105

Debriefing an Activity   107

Additional Resources   110
Index   111
Contributors   114
About the Author   115

Foreword

So, what's the most important asset in your organization?

People! The explosion of books, articles and periodicals devoted to "knowledge management" makes this clear. People make the best technology work, and people need to change with the marketplace and stay close to the customer.

When you have two or more people working together, you have a team. Some teams are functional, but many aren't. The best teams need to change the pace – and perhaps play – from time to time, and a boost of energy can help dysfunctional teams learn to work together.

Team Energizers will take your team to another level. Its ideas and strategies aren't theoretical (though they are based on sound theory!), but are crafted from the most important kind of testing: actual use with real people in the workplace.

Read this book with a highlighter and tape flags. Mark the ideas you can use with your teams, and then use at least one today. Keep this book out on your desk for the next 60 days as a reminder. Do something to energize and keep your teams energized every day!

May 2002

Bob Pike, CSP, CPAE Speakers Hall of Fame
Founder/Editor of The Creative Training Techniques newsletter
Chairman/CEO, The Bob Pike Group

Acknowledgements

This book is truly a team effort that evolved over the past ten years. I have been blessed with many people who have inspired and contributed to these team activities that I use in my facilitation practice.

I also thank my family and friends who graciously allow me experiment, play with and refine new Team Energizer ideas.

Preface

An icebreaker or "warm-up" is a wonderful technique to start a meeting. If done properly, these team activities create an energizing environment, enhance the team's work, and get people acquainted, talking and involved.

Some people love to start with icebreakers, while others want to dive right into the content of the meeting. So, when you do warm-ups, follow these guidelines for success:

Make it quick. Especially the first few times you do a team activity, make sure it lasts no more than five minutes. If your meeting is more than an hour long, you can increase the time accordingly.

Involve everyone. Make sure the activity has everyone actively involved. This means no wallflowers — everyone has something to do or is expected to contribute in some way. If in a very large group, create smaller teams or "break out groups" that allow everyone to interact and participate in the discussion.

Make it okay to pass. Some people may not want to participate — for whatever reason. In the introduction, tell your teammates they can say "pass" if they don't want to participate.

Be relevant. Most folks will go along with the activity if it has some relevance to the team's work. Introduce the icebreaker, why you chose that activity and what the benefits are — especially if the activity is a game or is unusual.

Be appropriate. Select an activity that will work with your team's preferences and styles, education level and background. For example, the Deck of Cards is a great activity for analytical types and miserable for those with no patience for numbers and statistics! The activity must also be appropriate for you to do with the group. If you don't like it, it's guaranteed they won't like it either!

Keep it simple. Many teams start out with an easy icebreaker where a question is asked and then each team member answers the question. For example: "Share with us the best team you have ever been on" and then each member answers the question (see Team Starters). Initially, stay away from "getting to know you/what's your hobby" perfunctory questions and those that require elaborate rules and explanations. As the team matures, you may try more personal or elaborate activities.

Be prepared. Practice the icebreaker in advance with your family or friends to make sure you understand the rules! Bring instructions, handouts or supplies with you and set up the space appropriately. When it's time, move quickly into a crisp explanation of the rules. (It's always a nice touch to post the key rules on an easel chart for all to see.) Make sure everyone understands the rules and process before you allow them to begin.

Be flexible. Adapt the activity to meet the needs of your team. Even though you have prepared yourself with a "dry run," the activity may not go as planned. That's okay; go with it! There's always a learning point – even if the activity is an utter failure in your eyes, debrief the activity in a very real and genuine way. You and your team will learn from the mistake.

Keep it lively. After the team has done a few easy icebreakers, try a different type of activity. There are dozens of books on icebreakers, warm-ups, team activities and games (like this one!) that may inspire you to try something different. If you want to encourage flexibility of mind, look for imaginative or creative activities.

Enjoy yourself. If you are looking forward to the warm-up, then others will too. Keep a sense of humor, and don't take side comments too personally.

Debrief the activity. Take a moment to apply the activity to the team's work. Ask the team, "What happened? What did you learn? How does it relate to the team's work? What's next or is there something we need to do to?" (see page 107 for more details).

Thank them. At the conclusion of the activity, thank everyone for participating and continue with the agenda.

After a while, the team will expect these icebreakers and you can experiment with the length, content and different methods. Encourage other team members to bring in new team activities and build the team! You'll find that team members learn from each other what they like and dislike, what works and what doesn't and how they work together as individuals and as a team.

This book contains fifty team activities that have a direct tie to the team's work. Most of them are quick and fun to do, even for the most intolerant of teams! The key is to "dry run" the activity on your family and friends. Learn what to do, what to expect and how to be comfortable with the activity. If you have fun with it, then the team will have fun and learn a few things too!

March 2003   Kristin J. Arnold
                                                                    Fairfax, VA

1. Aardvark and Antelope

Objective

To creatively demonstrate the idea that we can't rely on the team leader/expert to make all the decisions

Team Size

8 to 20 people

Time Required

10 to 15 minutes, depending on team size

Materials

- ❑ Two different colored marking pens
- ❑ One aardvark and one antelope stuffed animal (optional)

Physical Setting

A space large enough for the team to sit in a circle or U-shape

Process

Introduce the person at the end of the "U" or one person in the circle as the "fount of all knowledge about aardvarks." Hand that person a marker or the aardvark stuffed animal. "Whenever anyone needs to know anything about aardvarks, they have to come to Jane, oh fount of all knowledge about aardvarks."

Introduce the person at the other end of the "U" or the person sitting next to the "fount of all knowledge about aardvarks" as the "fount of all knowledge about antelopes." Hand that person a different colored marker. Restate, "Whenever anyone needs to know anything about antelopes, they have to come to Bob, oh fount of all knowledge about antelopes."

Explain to the team the rules of the activity: "This is how it works: Jane, you tell the person next to you (not Bob, the other person, Sally), 'This marker is an aardvark.' Sally, because she is NOT the fount of all knowledge asks Jane, 'A what?' Jane replies, 'An aardvark.' Sally then understands, and takes the marker from Jane."

Now Sally needs to explain the aardvark to the next person in the line, Kelly. But Sally is NOT the fount of all knowledge. She has to go back to the fount of all knowledge (Jane) and ask "A what?" To which Jane will reply "an aardvark." Sally will then tell Kelly, "It's an aardvark." And so the process begins. The only person who can verify that it is, in fact, an aardvark is Jane.

Same thing holds true for Bob and the antelopes. Make sure both "sides" understand the rules before you continue.

Now here is where the fun starts. The goal is to ensure that Bob (at the other end of the "U") understands about aardvarks and that Jane understands about antelopes. Pass the marker down the line, recognizing that you need to have the founts of all knowledge verify each time it passes from one team member to the next.

Then stand back and watch the confusion, especially when the two pens intersect in the midway point. They will be VERY confused!

Debrief and Summarize

After the aardvark and antelope have made it all the way around, debrief this activity with the following questions:

- What do you think about the founts of all knowledge?
- Was it necessary to keep going back to them?
- Do you see this dynamic on our team?
- How can we prevent this dynamic from occurring?

2. Active Listening

Objective

  To demonstrate the key elements to active listening

Team Size

  Groups of 5 to 6 people

Time Required

  15 to 20 minutes, depending on team size

Materials

  ❑ Marking pen

Physical Setting

  A space large enough for each group to sit
  in a circle

Process

  Whether your team is actively engaged in a "hot topic" or you want to use this as a learning activity, introduce this activity as a way to demonstrate "active listening."

  First, select a "hot topic" – one that is relevant and that will have some people agree and disagree (e.g., gun control, abortion, casual dress policies, or Internet use in the workplace).

  Pick up a marker and state, "He or she who has the pen has the 'floor.' The 'speaker' will tell their teammates his/her opinion about the hot topic. No one is to interrupt the speaker until the speaker is finished.

  "The 'listeners' are to listen, without interruption. Before anyone else may speak, one of the listeners must paraphrase the speaker. The speaker then decides whether the listener accurately captured his/her intent *and* the feeling.

  ♦ "If yes, then the speaker hands the marker to the person who
     accurately paraphrased him/her.
  ♦ "If no, then another person attempts to paraphrase the speaker.

  "You will continue this process until all have had a chance to speak."

Debrief and Summarize

  After all have had a chance to participate, debrief the activity:

  ♦ What did you think about this activity? Was it easy to do? If not, what
     made it so difficult?
  ♦ From the speakers' perspectives, what made you think you were
     listened to?
  ♦ From the listeners' perspectives, what made you a better listener?

- What did your fellow team members do to help you listen more effectively?
- What did your fellow team members to do help you speak more clearly?
- What did you learn from this activity? How might we apply these learnings to our team's work?

From your specific observations as well as the discussion, summarize the activity with the following key elements to active listening:

- **Prepare to listen.** Shift your focus and attention to the person speaking. Send a non-verbal signal (like turning your head toward the speaker) that you are giving that person your undivided attention.
- **Actively listen.** Listen with the intent to understand the speaker's words, putting aside your own agenda and immediate response.
- **Listen for meaning.** Use all your senses to take in information. Listen not only with your ears, but also with your eyes and heart. Take in the non-verbals, the tone, the pace and feel what the other person is saying.
- **Interpret the message.** As we take in all this information, focus on understanding what the speaker intends. Put yourself in their position. Be aware of your own values and beliefs that act as filters between the speaker's message and our interpretation. Resist the temptation to advise, criticize or judge when listening and asking questions. Make a conscious effort to understand other points of view.
- **Check for understanding.** Paraphrase or rephrase what was said and check for agreement.
- **Draw them out.** Ask open-ended questions to get more information.
- **Clarify as necessary.** Ask questions to gain a clearer understanding of what has been said, especially when you think there are differences in the way a word is used or defined.
- **Test the unsaid.** Sometimes, the real issue has not been spoken. If you sense there is something that hasn't been said, test it out.
- **Reflect the feeling.** This is the key to empathetic listening – where you seek to understand the speaker's feeling as well as the words.

3. Affinity Nametag

Objective
> To creatively demonstrate the use of the affinity diagram "tool"

Team Size
> 10 to 30 people

Time Required
> 15 to 20 minutes, depending on team size

Materials
> ❑ Label nametags
> ❑ Pen

Physical Setting
> A space large enough for the team to mingle about and gather in a large circle

Process
> Before you begin your team's brainstorming and affinity diagram session, introduce this activity as a fun, creative way to demonstrate how the affinity diagram works. Begin by handing out one nametag to each team member. Ask them to privately write down the name of a famous person – alive or dead, real or fictional.

> Once they have each written down a name, ask them to place the nametag on the *back* of the person sitting to their right. (Keep in mind that if you are sitting in any type of configuration other than circular, you may have to walk the end person's nametag over to the "first" person.)

> Ask the team members if they remember the game "Twenty Questions." Explain the directions by saying, "This step is the same as 'Twenty Questions' in that you can ask only close-ended questions of your teammates until you guess the right name. Once you have guessed the correct name on your nametag, move the nametag from your back to your front." Encourage mingling and asking different people different questions.

> After five minutes, if you still have some team members with nametags on their backs, tell the team members to offer a "clue." Within two minutes, all team members should have the nametags on their front.

> Explain to the team they now have a "brainstorm list" of famous people. Now they will do the "silent sort" – the real power of the affinity diagram. Ask the team members to silently move next to the famous person that they think they have an "affinity" with, or with whom they have something in common.

Allow the team to "silent sort" (you may have to reinforce the silence with a few "shhhhhs"). When they are close to being done (this should only take a minute or two), start humming the Jeopardy theme song, and when done, don't allow them to move from the cluster.

Once the song ends, tell them to look around and see if there is a better "fit" for them. It's okay to move from one "cluster" of famous people to another "cluster." If team members don't think they have anything in common, assure them that it is okay to "stand alone."

Go to each cluster and ask them for a word, phrase or statement that captures the flavor of the famous people in that cluster.

Debrief and Summarize

Summarize by restating the cluster "headers" and the idea that they took a brainstormed list of famous people and very quickly grouped them into creative, innovative clusters.

- ♦ How can we apply this to our current situation?
- ♦ When should we use this tool in future situations?

4. Assigning Priority: Make It All Fit

Objective

To creatively demonstrate the importance of prioritizing

Team Size

Any

Time Required

10 minutes

Materials

- ❑ One tennis ball and container
- ❑ Five golf balls
- ❑ A Ziploc® bag of black-eyed peas

Physical Setting

A space large enough for each team member to see the others

Process

Introduce this activity as a way to demonstrate the importance of prioritizing items.

Ask if anyone likes to play tennis and gently throw the tennis ball to one team member.

Ask if anyone likes to play golf and carefully throw a golf ball to five different team members. (Note: If your aim is poor, simply hand the golf ball to five different team members!)

Ask if anyone likes black-eyed peas and ask the team member to hold the bag of peas.

Explain to the team members that the tennis ball is your "A" task – absolutely vital and must be done; the golf balls are your "B" tasks – important and should be done; and the peas are your "C" tasks – they could be done. We call these the fast and friendlies.

Now when we start (our day/to execute our plan), where do we start? We start with the fast and friendlies.... (Hold the tennis ball canister out to the team member with the peas and ask to pour some in the canister.) Then what do we do? (As the team says, A, B, or C, put the corresponding item in the canister. All the items will not fit in the canister).

But how *should* we start (our day/to execute our plan)? We start with the most important As (put the tennis ball in the canister), the Bs and then the Cs. And guess what? We can put all the items in the canister!

Debrief and Summarize

From your specific observations as well as the discussion, summarize this activity by emphasizing the importance of prioritizing in order to accomplish "more with less."

- ♦ How can we apply this to our current situation?
- ♦ When should we use this tool in future situations?

5. Brainstorming Variations

Objective
To "brainstorm" or generate ideas in a different, more creative manner

Team Size
Any

Time Required
5 to 10 minutes, depending on team size

Materials
- ❑ Easel
- ❑ Marking pens
- ❑ Pen
- ❑ Paper

Physical Setting
A space large enough for each team member to see the others and the easel

Process
Developed in the late 1930s by Alex F. Osborne to stimulate his advertising executives' creativity, brainstorming has blossomed across America's meeting rooms as a way to generate lots of ideas quickly. Once you have agreed on the topic (such as "ideas to solve our problem of xyz"), review these simple ground rules:

- ◆ All ideas are valid – even if it seems silly, strange or similar.
- ◆ To pass is okay; we'll continue until all pass.
- ◆ Quickly capture ideas on an easel chart so all can see.
- ◆ "Hitchhiking" or building on others' ideas is encouraged.
- ◆ No praise, no comments, no criticism.
- ◆ We'll continue until everyone is satisfied that all ideas are captured.

Variations
Analogy. The team pretends it is solving a problem for a similar situation. The emphasis here is that it may be necessary to focus on a related situation in order to clearly understand the problem.

Chain reaction. Have each team member write down at least one idea. Ask two people to read one of their ideas. The rest of the team discusses how to combine both ideas. Then have a third person read another idea. The team must then work that idea into the first combination. Continue until each team member has contributed to the idea.

Compressed. Each team member writes down on a sheet of paper as many ideas as possible in fifteen seconds. When the team leader calls "time," each member passes the sheet to the left, and then has fifteen seconds to write down on the new sheet as many new ideas as possible. The key is to build on or enhance on each other's ideas.

Freewheel. Anyone on the team can call out an idea, with one person capturing the ideas on an easel chart.

Idea quota. The team comes up with a certain number of ideas in a predetermined timeframe. (For example, twenty ideas in five minutes.) The key is to come up with all kinds of ideas, then go through the list and pick out the ones that make the most sense to focus on.

Inversion. The team comes up with ideas destined to ensure the failure of the project or perpetuate the problem. The key is that good solutions can sometimes result from focusing on opposite goals.

Keep it simple. "Keep It Simple" or "KISS" is the key to this brainstorming variation. Try describing the idea in simple words, without using jargon or acronyms.

Martian. The team comes up with the wildest or "most out there" ideas possible. The key is that wild ideas can be "tamed" to produce sensible solutions. One rule: any idea is fair game.

Round robin. The team leader goes around the table for each person to contribute a new idea, add to or "hitchhike" on a previous idea. Each person has the option to pass.

Slip. Each member writes down each of their ideas on a separate slip of paper, Post-It® or index card. The ideas are then collected and organized.

Visualization. Picture the project finished, the problem solved or the mission accomplished. Once the "end in mind" is firmly visualized in the mind's eye, work backward through every step needed to make it a reality.

Viva la difference. Consider looking at the problem from a different viewpoint. For instance, if the team is developing a marketing plan for a new product aimed at teenagers, how would that marketing plan look to a postage carrier? A teacher? A mother? By considering another point of view, your team can gain fresh insights into developing the plan.

Debrief and Summarize

After all have had a chance to participate, summarize this activity by recognizing all the wonderful ideas the team has generated. Get agreement on next steps to the process (e.g., a quick vote or categorize the information).

6. Break Out Groups

Objective
> To create sub-teams to encourage open communication, creativity, idea generation and independent thinking

Team Size
> Any

Time Required
> 1 to 3 minutes, depending on team size

Materials
> ❑ Various

Physical Setting
> A space large enough for the team to separate into smaller groups

Process

Not everything has to be done in a large team. Sometimes, it is preferable to break the larger team into sub-teams or break out groups to allow for:

- ♦ More detailed work to get done.
- ♦ More direct and intimate conversation.
- ♦ Relationships to form.
- ♦ More introverted team members to contribute.
- ♦ An infusion of energy by physically moving them around (especially in the afternoon).
- ♦ Teammates to get out of a rut of sitting next to the same people!

Get agreement from the team that the next piece of work should be done in smaller groups (or even an action item might be done by a smaller group).

Once you have agreement, there are several ways to break people up into smaller groups:

- ♦ **Ask for volunteers.** If in a large group, point to the four corners of the room and announce the different activities to work on and ask that folks move to the area they would like to work on. (Note, after everyone has moved, you may need to balance the groups.)

♦ **Self-select.** If working on the same issue, ask people to move into groups of no more than x number of people. If working on different issues, post the issues on an easel chart and ask them to move to the easel chart that interests them the most. (Note, you may have to do a bit of shuffling to balance the teams.)

♦ **Count off.** Ask the group to "count off" from one to x number of groups you want to have. Point to the area you want all the "ones" to meet, "twos" to meet, etc.

  o Count the total number of people you have (N).
  o Identify the number of people you want in each group (P).
  o Divide N by P and you have the number of groups you want (x).

♦ **Preselect.** Preassign a number, letter or color to each person on the nametags or name tents. When you need to break them into groups, ask for all the As to join together, all the Bs, etc.

♦ **Presorted toys.** Many teams keep koosh balls and other small toys on the tables. Place just enough toys that there is one for each person. Vary the toys so that they can be easily sorted. For example:

  o Small stuffed balls – football, soccer, basketball, hackysack etc.
  o Koosh balls – different colors.
  o Duplos or Legos – different colors and different sizes.

♦ **Physical characteristics.** Observe obvious physical characteristics that would allow you to break people into small groups. (Caution: make sure you won't offend anyone!). For example:

  o Clothing – people wearing blue shirts, brown shirts, light-colored shirts etc.
  o Gender – male, female.
  o Shoes – people wearing tennis shoes, sandals, oxfords etc.
  o Hair length – short, medium, long.
  o Pierced ears – those with and those without!

♦ **Stratified.** Separate the team based on some functional characteristic. For example:

  o Geography – where people live or work.
  o Work Unit – by work group, unit, department, division, organization, company etc.
  o Position – by grade level within the company such as employee, supervisor, manager, executive etc.
  o Age – Boomers, X-ers, etc.

Be clear about your expectations, the sub-team's deliverable, time frame and, if necessary, the process they should follow. Then, let 'em go for it!

7. Build an Agenda

Objective

To create an agenda when faced with a team that doesn't have clarity of purpose or process

Team Size

Any

Time Required

5 to 10 minutes

Materials

- ❑ Easel chart
- ❑ Marking pens

Physical Setting

A space large enough for each team member to see the others and the easel

Process

When there is no agenda, ask the team to build one! Before the team gets too involved in spinning its wheels, put your hand up and ask, "Where's the agenda?" If the other team members look at you with glazed eyes or eager expressions, take advantage of the situation. Quickly hop up out of your seat, grab a easelchart marker and ask, "What do we need to accomplish at this meeting?" Write down each idea *the way it was stated* and the name of the person who suggested the idea. Note: you are asking the team to identify outcomes or expected results – not just a laundry list of topics. Before you move on to the next step, ask if everyone understands the outcomes and clarify if necessary. Combine similar items. If there is any dissent, assume that the ideas are distinct and should remain separate. Elapsed time to list the outcomes: no more than five minutes.

Next, take each item and ask the suggestor how long it will take to achieve the outcome. If the team disagrees, allow a few seconds for discussion and write down the most agreed-upon time. Remember: an agenda is just a roadmap and the time limits are guideposts. If the team later agrees that they need more time, they will have the flexibility to adjust their agenda.

Ask the suggestors if they would like to lead the discussion. If not, then ask the team for a volunteer. Beware: if just one or two people are leading all the items, you'll end up with a one-way conversation! Elapsed time to identify time limits and leaders: two minutes.

Finally, prioritize your list. Most teams have too much to do and not enough time, so it is critical to start with the most important. (See team energizer #4, Assigning Priority, for another fun activity).

Some teams simply rank the agenda items with number one being the most important, two as the next most important, etc. Or try the ABC concept, where "A" is vital: we must accomplish this outcome at this meeting; "B" is important: we should accomplish this outcome; and "C" is trivial: we could do this, but the world won't come to an end if we don't accomplish this today. When prioritizing, quickly go through the list and ask "Is this an A, B or C?" and write down the most agreed-upon letter. Some teams continue to prioritize by sequencing each group of letters – identifying A1, A2, A3, B1, B2, B3, C1, C2, C3. Elapsed time: one or two minutes.

You have now built your agenda! Start with the A1, and move through the list. Total time: no more than ten minutes – a worthwhile investment to the team's work.

Debrief and Summarize
At the end of the team meeting, ask for feedback on the process. Did the agenda help or hinder the team?

Summarize by thanking your teammates for indulging your need to provide a bit of structure for your valuable time together!

8. Building an Extraordinary Team

Objective

To create a space for team discussion on strengths and opportunities for improvement

Team Size

Any

Time Required

20 to 30 minutes, depending on team size

Materials

- ❑ Easel paper
- ❑ Marking pens
- ❑ Red and green removable dots
- ❑ Prepared easel chart with characteristics written down the center

Physical Setting

A space large enough for each team member to see the others and the easel

Process

Introduce the concept of an extraordinary team — a high performance team that accomplishes the desired results quickly, efficiently and effectively. As each team journeys toward becoming a high-performance team, it should periodically pause and reflect on what's working well and how to improve.

Give each team member three green dots and three red dots. Caution them to listen carefully to the following characteristics, as they will be asked to place three green dots on the characteristics they believe the team does well and three red dots on those they believe the team can use some improvement.

Describe the following characteristics of an extraordinary team:

- ♦ **Clear goals.** Everyone understands the purpose and direction of the team. Everyone pulls in the same direction for success.
- ♦ **Shared roles.** Team task and maintenance roles are clearly defined and easily shared between team members. A key shared role is the team leader. The "leader" shares the responsibility and the glory, is supportive and fair, creates a climate of trust and openness, and is a good coach and teacher. The leadership role shifts at various times and, in the most productive teams, it is difficult to identify the leader during a casual observation.

15

- **Open and clear communication.** Poor listening, poor speaking, and the inability to provide constructive feedback can be major roadblocks to team progress. For success, team members must listen for meaning, speak with clarity, engage in dialogue and discussion, and provide continual feedback through the communication process.
- **Effective decision making.** The team is aware of and uses many methods to arrive at its decisions. Consensus is often touted as the best way to make decisions — and it is an excellent method — but the team should also use command decision, expert decision, majority vote, minority control, and command decision with input. Depending on the time available and the amount of commitment and resources required, a successful team selects the appropriate decision making method for each decision.
- **Valued diversity.** Members are valued for the unique contributions they bring to the team. A diversity of thinking, ideas, methods, experiences and opinions is encouraged. Whether you are creative or logical, fast or methodical, team members recognize each other's individual talents and tap their expertise — both job-related and other skills they bring to the team. Flexibility and sensitivity are key elements in appreciating these differences.
- **Conflict managed constructively.** Problems are not swept under the rug. Some may compete to have their opinions heard, while others may accommodate the stronger team members or avoid the conflict altogether. A successful team has discussed its philosophy about how to manage conflict and sees well-managed conflict as a healthy way to create new ideas and to solve difficult problems.
- **A cooperative climate.** The atmosphere encourages participation, trust and openness. Members of the team are equally committed and involved. They know they need each other's skills, knowledge and expertise to produce something together that they could not do separately. There is a sense of belonging and a willingness to make things work for the good of the whole team. People are comfortable enough with each other to be creative, take risks and make mistakes. It also means you hear plenty of laughter and the team members enjoy what they are doing.

Ask the team to place the dots on the appropriate characteristic (see "Red Dot, Blue Dot").

Debrief and Summarize

After all have placed their dots on the chart, debrief the results:

- What does this information tell us?
- What seem to be the strengths of the team?
- What seem to be the areas for improvement (recognizing that *all* teams can get better)?
- What are some of the things we can do to improve our teamwork?

9. Chain Story

Objective
> To encourage active listening and creativity

Team Size
> Groups of 6 to 10 people

Time Required
> 10 to 15 minutes, depending on team size

Materials
> ❑ Eight to ten various household objects, such as toys, sports equipment, a book or cooking utensils

Physical Setting
> A space large enough for the team to gather (sit or stand) around a table in the center

Process
> Display all the objects on the table, visible to all. Ask a volunteer to select one object and tell the team a short story about the object and take no longer than a minute.

> Ask another team member to select a second object and *continue* the story, tying in the new object into the story. Again, no longer than a minute.

> Continue until all objects have been selected and all team members have contributed to the story.

Debrief and Summarize
> After all have had a chance to participate, debrief the activity:

> ◆ What did you like about this activity?
> ◆ What made the story work?
> ◆ As individual contributors, what contributed to the success of the story?
> ◆ Did the team members help each other? How?
> ◆ What would have made the process work better?
> ◆ How might we apply these lessons to our team's work?

For more team energizers, go to:
www.QPCteam.com

10. Change!

Objective
> To demonstrate issues associated with change

Team Size
> Any

Time Required
> 10 minutes

Materials
> None

Physical Setting
> A space large enough to have the team to stand and "pair up" into groups of two

Process
> Introduce this activity as a way to demonstrate the effects of change. Ask the team members to stand up and find a partner.

> Tell them to look at their partner carefully. Then ask them to turn "back to back" and make five changes to their appearance. As a facilitator, you may want to pair up with someone to demonstrate your instructions. Typically, the group will be very quiet and intent on its task.

> After a minute, ask the team members to turn around, face each other, and identify the five changes to their appearance. At this point, you will probably hear lots of laughter! Roam around and ask how many changes the partners identified.

> Ask them to turn "back to back" and make eight more changes. You may hear some moans and groans, and some may even "check-out." That's okay!

> After a few minutes, ask them to turn around, face each other, and identify the eight changes. Roam around and ask how many changes were made and identified.

Debrief and Summarize

After all have had a chance to identify the changes, debrief the activity:

- Tell us what happened in this activity.

- How did you feel when asked to make eight additional changes? (Show them how easy it could be to "change your appearance" by picking up thirteen cents, or by picking up thirteen markers, etc. Team members will invariably respond by saying "You broke the rules!" You coyly respond, "What rules?")

- Ask if anyone "benchmarked" your (the facilitator's) demonstration. After all, the facilitator has been through the exercise before, and they should have observed what you did to make the changes!

From your specific observations as well as the discussion, summarize the key issues traditionally associated with change initiatives:

- People tend to focus inward when faced with change.
- People forget to look beyond themselves when faced with change issues – even when the answer is in plain sight.
- They also tend to impose boundaries and ground rules on themselves that don't really exist.
- Too much change frustrates people.
- People don't share their feelings when stressed by change.
- We make change too hard.

Conclude this activity by summarizing the key points. Ask them to be open-minded as they continue with their team's work.

Inspired by Larry Mercier

11. Check In and Check Out

Objective

To enable the team to "form" quickly, provide a sense of closure to the team's activities, and to let each other know what's going on with them personally

Team Size

Any

Time Required

5 to 10 minutes, depending on team size

Materials

❑ None

Physical Setting

A space large enough for the team to sit in a circle or U-shape

Process

People come to a team meeting with all kinds of random thoughts – what work still needs to be done, a problem to be solved, and a rumor floating around the coffee pot. They aren't really focused on the task to be accomplished or the process that will be used.

What they usually do is stroll in, check out who's there, and maybe engage in light conversation with one or two people before getting down to business. Take advantage of this natural "check in" with one or two people to "check in" with the team. It allows team members to share what's on their minds so they can focus on the team's work.

At the beginning of each team meeting, just ask, "How's it going?" or "What's been going on since we last met?" It allows people to share what's going on with them personally as well as organizationally.

When you allow people a few moments up front to share issues or "get it off their chest," it allows people to be physically and mentally present with the team.

Check off each block when you hear these words during a meeting, seminar, or phone call. When you get five blocks horizontally, vertically, or diagonally, stand up and shout **BINGO!**

B	I	N	G	O
		Win-Win		

12. Cliché BINGO

Objective

To inject some laughter in an otherwise dry meeting and keep the team's attention

Team Size

Any

Time Required

2 minutes of explanation

Materials

- ❑ Prepared BINGO cards (see previous page)
- ❑ Pens
- ❑ M&Ms®, Skittles® or other candy game pieces (optional)

Physical Setting

A space large enough for each team member to see the others

Process

Create a "BINGO card" for each team member. (For teams who are used to working with each other and have developed their own team terminology, you can hand out the card and ask them to fill in the blanks with their own words.)

At the beginning of the meeting, hand out the Cliché BINGO cards to each team member. Ask the team members to check off words as they are used in the team meeting. (Note: you cannot check off a word you used – it has to be said by someone else.) When someone checks off five words in a row – horizontal, vertical or diagonal – yell out "BINGO!"

Debrief and Summarize

At the end of the team meeting, debrief the activity:

- ♦ How do these clichés add value to the conversation?
- ♦ How did this game affect your use (or decision not to use) these clichés?
- ♦ How might we apply these lessons to our team's work?

Variation

You can also add a bit of sugar to the mix with some M&Ms® or Skittles® to help the team check off their words!

To make your own, distinctive BINGO cards, fill each box with a team cliché such as:

- At the End of the Day
- Ball Park
- Benchmark
- Best Practice
- Bottom Line
- Core Competencies
- Customer-Driven
- Customer Focus(ed)
- Empower
- Fast Track
- Game Plan
- Go the Extra Mile

- Hardball
- Infusion
- Knowledge Base
- Leverage
- Low Hanging Fruit
- Mindset
- Movers and Shakers
- Out of the Loop
- Paradigm Shift
- Proactive
- Put This One to Bed
- Results-Driven
- Revisit

- Slippery Slide
- Strategic Fit
- Stretch the Envelope
- Synergy
- Take that Offline
- Think Outside the Box
- The Big Picture
- Total Quality
- Touch Base
- Turn the Corner
- 24/7
- Value Added
- Win-Win

Feel free to add your own clichés, search at www.buzzwhack.com or borrow some from Dilbert®! Don't forget to make the space in the middle of each sheet a "free space." Note: if you don't want everyone to have the same BINGO card, you can make several versions with different words.

24

13. Decisions, Decisions

Objective

To demonstrate the team process of making decisions – especially with new team members who don't know each other well

Team Size

Groups of 3 to 5 people

Time Required

20 minutes

Materials

- ❑ Prepared 5″x7″ index cards with the name of the city, length of stay, travel time and cost
- ❑ Map of vacation destination and/or travel brochure

Physical Setting

A space large enough for groups to collaborate

Process

Begin by painting the picture of your team traveling to an exotic destination (e.g., Italy). The challenge is that all team members must agree on the itinerary within the following constraints:

- ♦ You only have ten days total.
- ♦ You must arrive and depart from Rome (or other central destination).
- ♦ The possibilities are described on the provided index cards (hand out the cards...noting the actual time at the location as well as the travel time to get there).
- ♦ Total amount budgeted for travel and lodging is $5,000.

This will be their starting point. Indicate on each card the minimum amount of time that they must stay in whatever cities they choose and the travel time (in days) from the arrival point to the other cities. Determine how many days the vacation will last. Inform the team that it has ten minutes to decide how to spend its ten-day vacation.

Ask each team to share its travel itinerary.

Debrief and Summarize

After each team has shared the travel itineraries, debrief the activity:

- ◆ How did your team make decisions?
- ◆ Did the team have a consensus? If not, what kind of decisions were made?
- ◆ What worked well for the team?
- ◆ What would have made the process work better?
- ◆ Did the team "think out of the box?" (e.g., asking the facilitator if they could take more travel time by traveling by a slower mode or if they could allow "fluid" time so that they could stay longer in a city than planned.)
- ◆ What did you learn from this activity?
- ◆ How might we apply these lessons to our team's work?

Inspired by Sally Holloway

14. The Deck of Cards: A Variation of Deming's Funnel Experiment[1]

Objective
To demonstrate the harmful effects of overadjusting a process

Team Size
4 groups of 3 to 5 people

Time Required
30 minutes

Materials
- ❑ One pack of playing cards per team
- ❑ Four tape measurers
- ❑ Four colored dots to serve as the "target" – one colored dot for each team
- ❑ A dozen colored dots of a different color to serve as the last targeted position for Team B
- ❑ "Rule cards" for each team, located in the back of this book
- ❑ A data collection form for each team (optional)

Physical Setting
A room large enough for four teams of people to stand and work in small circles. Place a colored dot in the center of each of the four teams

Process
Prior to the session, place the one colored dot or "target" on the floor where each of the four teams will be centered around for this activity.

Divide the team members into four teams. Tell them to group themselves around the dots on the floor, or "targets."

Tell the teams that the objective of this exercise is to produce as many products as close to the target as possible, while following their particular "rule." Hold up the four cards for all to see.

Tell the teams that they produce product by dropping one playing card from shoulder height. Demonstrate dropping the card – drop the card perpendicular (not horizontal) to the colored dot or "target" on the floor; this provides the most variation!

---

[1] Deming, W.E. (1986). *Out of the Crisis*. Cambridge, MA: MIT Press.

Reiterate the goal: to produce as many products as close to the target as possible, while following their particular rule. Hand out one deck of playing cards, tape measurer and one "rule card" to each team. Go over the rules for each team:

Team A: Don't adjust. Drop every card over the target.

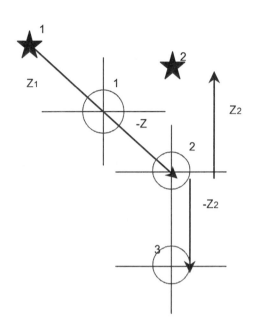

Team B: After each drop, measure the distance (z) from the target to the spot ★ where the card landed. Set the next drop position over the point (-z) from *the last targeted position*. Use the additional colored dots to mark your last targeted position.

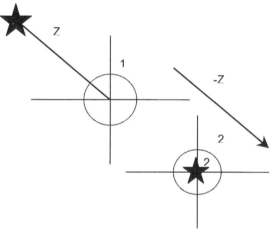

Team C: After each drop, measure the distance (z) from the target to the spot ★ where the card landed. Set the next drop position over the point (-z) *from the target* (same distance, but opposite direction).

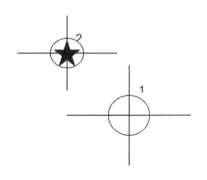

Team D: Set the next drop position right over the spot ★ where the last dropped card landed.

Allow the teams to produce a dozen or so products. Pay particular attention to teams B and C; their rules are the toughest to follow.

Debrief and Summarize

After all have finished dropping at least twelve cards, review the distribution of cards with the entire group:

- ♦ Ask the team to share the rule it followed.
- ♦ Ask the team to share the results and speculate what happened to its process.
- ♦ Ask the team to share an example of where it sees the same type of pattern happening.

 Team A: The cards will tend to be **clustered** around the target. The distribution is stable with minimum variation around the target. Even if you have a bad process, you'll get an even distribution. This is a stable process, and by far, the best choice.

Team B: The variation explodes and is unstable but symmetrical around the target, as we **tamper** with the process. The operator knows where the standard is, but adjusts based on the last piece produced – and where he or she thinks it should be. Like setting an oven to bake a cake, if we know from past experience that the oven was too hot, we'll adjust the control to be a smidgen less than it was when we baked our cake before.

Team C: The distribution explodes in opposite directions, as we  **overcompensated** for our errors. This is the way most processes are overadjusted from where the operation was during the last process run. Like a novice driver steering a car, the operator overadjusts (or management overreacts!).

Team D: The cards will tend to **drift**. The distribution is unstable and moves away from the target in one direction. This is the kind of process drift that can occur when we use the last piece produced as the standard for the next piece, instead of a universal product standard. Drifting also occurs when we let experienced employees "show the ropes" to new employees, without any training standard.

Have each team come up with its own examples of losses in its organization resulting from Rules B, C and D. If possible, ask the team members to estimate the losses to the organization.

Close with a discussion of how organizations take a stable process and try to make it better. The result of our efforts will only make it worse – double the variance or cause the process to explode. What is required is a fundamental change in the system.

Important! You will want to do a dry run of this activity. Make sure you understand the four rules!

Variation

If time permits, do another "round," allowing the teams to make process improvements. Have each team identify one improvement to make, test it, and then compare the results. For example, one process improvement might be to hold the card parallel to the floor before dropping it. The result using Rule A will be that almost every card will settle down on top of the target!

Inspired by W. Edwards Deming and Steve Holcomb
© 2001 American Society for Quality

15. Face the Facts

Objective

To allow team members who work virtually or on different shifts to get to know each other

Team Size

Any

Time Required

Initially, an hour or so to set this up

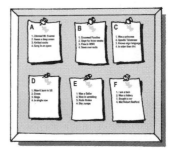

Materials Required

- ❑ Camera
- ❑ Bulletin board (real or virtual)
- ❑ Index cards
- ❑ Ballots
- ❑ Prize

Physical Setting

A centrally located bulletin board

Process

Ask each team member for a recent picture or take a picture of each team member. In addition, ask each team member for three unknown or little-known facts about themselves that they are willing to share with their teammates.

Edit the facts for grammar or obvious identifying characteristics, and then write the facts on an index card. Post the pictures on one side of a bulletin board, and the cards on the other side, NOT in the same order. Label the pictures A, B, C... and the facts 1, 2, 3....

Tell the team it has a set amount of time (e.g., one month) to match correctly the pictures (the letters) with the facts (the numbers). Instruct the team members to submit the results on a "ballot" or use email if working virtually. Award prizes to the first three members who successfully complete this activity.

Inspired by Brother Richard Dube

For more team energizers, go to:
www.QPCteam.com

16. Follow the Process

Objective
To demonstrate the importance of clear process instructions

Team Size
Any

Time Required
5 minutes

Materials
- Colorful sheet of paper for each team member

Physical Setting
A space large enough for the team to be able to see the person giving the instructions

Process
Give each person one sheet of colorful paper (e.g., fluorescent yellow paper). As the instructor, do not pick up a piece of paper – or else the team members will pick up the paper in the same direction you do!

Ask the team to follow your directions:

"First, please close your eyes."

"Please fold your paper in half." Note: some team members may want to question you, but don't answer them. Just repeat your instruction. Once they have completed the procedure, move on to the next instruction:

"Please tear off the upper right hand corner of your paper."

"Fold the paper in half again."

"Please tear off the lower left hand corner."

"Fold the paper in half once again."

"Please tear off the upper right hand corner."

When all have completed this last instruction, ask the team members to open their eyes and open their papers. Look shocked, absolutely shocked at the different results. Hint: some papers will have one, two or three holes in the middle of the paper, etc.

In a middle-manager questioning tone ask, "What happened? I gave pretty specific instructions – and yet you came up with different results!" Let the team tell you what went wrong, for example:

♦ You didn't let us ask questions/answer our questions.
♦ We couldn't see what others were doing.
♦ We didn't know what you wanted or what the end product was.

Agree that you probably could have done a better job communicating the instructions.

Debrief and Summarize

From your specific observations as well as the discussion, debrief the activity:

♦ What would have helped to make the instructions better and receive a more consistent result?
♦ Do you see this dynamic on teams?
♦ How can we prevent this dynamic from occurring?
♦ How might we apply these lessons to our team's work?

17. Gordian Knot

Objective

To creatively demonstrate problem-solving skills

Team Size

Group(s) of 5-15 people

Time Required

10 to 15 minutes, depending on team size

Materials

❑ None

Physical Setting

A space large enough for the team/groups to stand in circle(s)

Process

Introduce this activity as a method to demonstrate problem-solving techniques with a "Gordian Knot" and share the story of the Gordian Knot:

According to Greek legend, the Oracle prophesized that the next king of Phrygia would arrive by oxcart. Gordius and his wife came strolling into town, and Gordius was made king. In gratitude, Gordius dedicated his oxcart to Zeus, tying it with an intricate knot to a pole in the public square. The oracle declared that anyone who succeeded in untying the knot would be the conqueror of all Asia.

Many years passed, and the knot stayed tied until Alexander the Great traveled to Phrygia. Alexander attempted to untie the knot like everyone else. When it became apparent that conventional means wouldn't work, he drew his sword and sliced the knot in half. Hence, "cutting the Gordian knot" came to mean solving a difficult problem.

Let the team know that they will be solving a difficult "knotty" problem of their own! Ask the team members to gather around in a circle, so that people are standing shoulder to shoulder. (You may also warn them that you won't be asking them to sing *Kum-by-ya* anytime soon!)

If any women are wearing high heels, ask them to remove their shoes.

Ask each person to stick out one hand and "shake" or "grab" just one other person's hand – not standing beside him or her. Walk around the group(s) and make sure it is just one hand connecting to one other hand – not a five-hand pile-up!

Ask the group to take their other hand and "shake" or "grab" another person's hand. Again, emphasize one hand connecting to just one other hand.

Ask the team to "untangle" itself – in other words, to make the circle "bigger" without breaking the connections between the hands (or pulling out a sword to slice the knot in half).

Then stand back and watch the fun!

Most teams are able to figure it out; either they untangle themselves into one large circle or two or three interconnected circles. A true "Gordian" knot cannot be untied.

Debrief and Summarize

After each team has had a chance to untangle themselves, debrief the activity:

- ♦ What worked well for your teams?
- ♦ How did team members help each other?
- ♦ How did you go about solving your problem?
- ♦ What did you have to do differently to solve your problem?
- ♦ What did you learn from this activity?
- ♦ How might we apply these lessons to our team's work?

18. The Hats We Wear

Objective

To demonstrate the concept of informal roles and how it affects the team dynamic and decision-making process

Team Size

6 or more people

Time Required

30 minutes

Materials

- ❑ List of items that can be prioritized
- ❑ Six baseball caps with the following printed on the front of each cap:
    - ♦ Obey me
    - ♦ Ask my opinion
    - ♦ Ask my opinion, but ignore it
    - ♦ Ignore me
    - ♦ Laugh at me
    - ♦ (Nothing)

Hint: You can print these easily on index cards and tape the card to the front of each hat or print the caps with liquid paint.

Physical Setting

Six chairs placed in a circle with the "observers" standing or sitting around the outside of the circle

Process

Begin with a list of approximately ten items that need to be prioritized. Note: you may have to put together a list, based on previous team discussions, but make sure that the list is meaningful and relevant to the team.

Ask the team members to individually rank the importance of each item from one to ten with one being the most important to ten being the least important.

When the team members have completed their individual ranking, ask for six volunteers. Ask them to bring their chairs and sit in the center of the team. Ask those who remain to be process observers and watch how this team of six individuals accomplishes its task.

Ask the team of six, "Please reach agreement on the priority of the listed items. You have ten minutes to accomplish this task. However, before you start, you must follow a few ground rules. I have six hats that I will place on your head. Please do not take them off until I tell you that you can. For those of you who are looking at these hats, please follow the instructions to whatever extent you choose. Process Observers – please watch how the team achieves its objective. You have ten minutes."

The team will be very uncomfortable and probably ask you for clarification. Simply repeat the ground rules.

After ten minutes, if the team has not finished, allow thirty seconds to finish. (Note, do NOT let them look at their hats!)

Debrief and Summarize

After the group has prioritized the list, ask for the "final product/list" that the team agrees to.

Ask the team member with the loudest complaint what they don't like about it. Individually debrief each team member wearing a hat *without letting them look at the hats* until told to do so:

- Do you like the list? What do you like/don't like about it?
- Process observers: What did you see this team member do?
- Do you know what is on your hat? (If they say no, press them for an answer!)
- Ask the team member to look at the hat. Are you surprised?
- What did you think of the process used?

Note: Save the team member wearing the hat with nothing printed on it for last. This team member will think that there is something on it - reemphasizing the point that we all come together with "hats" on.

Debrief the entire team:

- What do think about this activity?
- What do you think about the hats we wear when come together on a team?
- How do our hats affect our decision-making process?
- Do you see this dynamic on our team?
- How can we prevent this dynamic from occurring?
- How might we be able to help each other when we see this dynamic occurring?

19. H-O-M-E-S Is Where the Heart Is

Objective

To develop quicker recall of specific, job-related information

Team Size

Groups of 5 to 6 people

Time Required

15 to 20 minutes, depending on team size

Materials

- ❑ 3″ x 5″ cards
- ❑ Pens

Physical Setting

Ideally, the room is set up with table groupings for five or six team members

Process

Whether the team is dealing with information overload, productivity issues, stress, presentations, or the need to develop greater memory power, this activity illustrates how the development of a personalized mnemonic device can lead to greater self-confidence and efficiency.

Begin with the illustration of the word "H-O-M-E-S," which provides an excellent trigger for remembering the names of the Great Lakes: Huron, Ontario, Michigan, Erie, Superior. Ask team members to list at least one thing that, when quickly recalled, could make their job easier. Each entry should be detailed on a separate 3″ x 5″ card. The item could be as simple as a phone number or as complicated as names of tenants in a building.

Collect the cards, shuffle them, and distribute two or three to each team with this charge: "You are to come up with a mnemonic device that will help the person who wrote this remember it more rapidly." Encourage alliterative, rhyming, melodic and graphic representations.

Call on a spokesperson from each team to describe the device they came up with. Ask for feedback from the person who submitted the original list on the 3″ x 5″ card.

Debrief and Summarize

After all have had a chance to participate, debrief the activity:

- What are the advantages to having an excellent memory?
- What things do you do to develop your memory?
- What memory aids does your team currently employ?
- How might we apply these lessons to our team's work?

Contributed by Dr. Marlene Caroselli

20. The Huddle

Objective

To allow team members to resolve issues between just a few team members – and not the entire team

Team Size

Any

Time Required

5 to 15 minutes, depending on team size

Materials

❑ None

Physical Setting

A space large enough for the team to mingle about

Process

Whether you use this activity as an icebreaker or at the conclusion of your team meeting, suggest a "huddle" with the following ground rules:

- ◆ **One on one.** Use this time to meet with one or two team members that you need to ask a question, resolve an issue, share an idea, etc. Avoid discussing agenda items that should involve the entire team.

- ◆ **Be brief.** It's a quick time to check calendars, update each other and quickly share information. If you need more time, agree on a specific time to get together.

- ◆ **Stay here.** Don't leave the room. Be available to each other to "huddle." If you must leave, come back as soon as possible.

- ◆ **Be polite.** If your team members are talking, wait patiently until they are done. Remember, they will be brief!

- ◆ **Focus on team business.** Socializing is acceptable, but not encouraged. Those having business issues can freely interrupt social activity.

- ◆ **End on time.** The timekeeper will call "break" when the huddle is over.

Debrief and Summarize

When finished with the huddle, recommend that other unfinished business be taken up after the team meeting. You may also ask for feedback on the process. Did the huddle help or hinder the team's work?

21. Johari Window

Objective

To creatively discuss the importance of team building activities and feedback

Team Size

5 to 30 people

Time Required

15 to 20 minutes, depending on team size

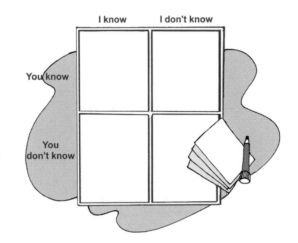

Materials

- ❑ Easel paper with "window" drawn without the labels
- ❑ Marking pen
- ❑ Paper for each team member
- ❑ Pens

Physical Setting

A space large enough for the team to mingle about and gather in a circle

Process

Describe the elements of the Johari Window, while writing the elements on the easel chart:

- ◆ "There are things you know about me, and I know about me. This is called my 'open window.'" Ask for examples of things the team knows about you and that you know about yourself (e.g., I have two children. I live in Virginia).

- ◆ "There are things I know about myself that you don't know about me. Some of these things you will never, ever know. This is called my 'hidden window.' However, as you get to know me, I let you know more things about me. I let down my 'façade' and move things from my hidden window into the open window. Icebreakers such as these help us get to know each other better."

- ◆ "There are things you know about me that I just don't know about myself. Like that poppy seed that got stuck between my teeth at lunch. I may not know it's there, until I go home and look in the mirror and gasp 'I have a poppy seed stuck between my teeth! How 'come nobody told me?' This is where the power of feedback is so important in teams. Both positive as well as constructive feedback."

- "But the really exciting thing is this last window, where both you and I don't know what we know. This is the window of the 'creative unknown'. A very exciting place to be! But notice, we can't tap into the team synergy without team activities and feedback. So let's do a fun activity that leverages our creative unknown."

Ask each team member to write his or her name on the top. Then ask everyone to pass the paper to the person to your right.

Ask each team member to write the name of a movie, TV show, book or magazine that somehow describes the named person.

When the paper has been circulated to every member on the team, ask each team member to read his or her paper aloud. Team members may agree or act surprised at the comments.

Debrief and Summarize
After each team member has read the paper aloud, remark that we have just given feedback through a team activity! Debrief the activity:

- What did you like most about this activity?
- Which windows opened for you?
- Which is easier, to give or receive feedback?
- How can giving feedback contribute to the team dynamic?
- How can giving feedback hurt the team dynamic?
- How might we apply this concept to the team?

22. Juggling Priorities

Objective

To introduce the context of balancing life and juggling priorities while introducing team members to each other

Team Size

Groups of 5 to 15 people

Time Required

15 to 20 minutes, depending on team size

Materials

- ❑ A watch
- ❑ A bag for the objects or big pockets
- ❑ Five different objects to juggle, including a ball of yarn

Hint: Objects should be of differing size, shape and weight. Avoid hard objects that may injure team members or round objects that will roll away from the group.

Physical Setting

A space large enough for each group to stand in a circle

Process

Ask the team members to stand in a circle shoulder-width apart from each other.

With the objects in your pocket or in an opaque bag, explain the rules:

- ◆ Say a person's name first, and then throw the object to that person. The catcher will say "Thank you, (name of the thrower)" to the thrower. The catcher says another person's name and throws the object to a new catcher, who continues to say "Thank you, (name of the thrower)".
- ◆ Once a person has caught and thrown the object, he or she folds their arms across the chest to indicate they already had a turn.
- ◆ The group will continue the process until the last team member throws the object back to the facilitator.

Start the process and continue one round. After one round, ask the team members to stand on one leg if physically able.

Begin round two with the team members standing on one leg. Repeat the process with the object thrown around the circle in exactly the same order as before. When the object returns to you, continue to throw it to the first catcher for a second time around the circle, continuing to state the name and saying thank you.

After the object is approximately one person beyond the first catcher, throw another object (#2) into the circle to the first catcher.

After object #2 is approximately one person beyond the first catcher, then object #3 is introduced to the first catcher. Continue to introduce objects until all are in play.

Continue throwing around the circle until the object #5 comes back to you. Once all the objects have been around the circle once, hold onto the objects and stop the process when you have all the objects.

Debrief and Summarize

When you once again have all the objects, debrief the activity:

- What happened?
- Who stood on only one leg for the entire time as I asked? If you didn't, why not?
- How did you compensate for not being able to hold your leg up? Did you use your teammates for support or other sources?
- Did you practice self-policing? Did you decide that you could be more productive doing it your own way instead of how you were told to do it?
- Was anybody cheating? How we play is typically how we work.
- Were you more or less productive on one or two legs? (People usually find they are more productive when balanced. If unbalanced, it is hard to handle their priorities and they tend to drop the ball.)
- What happened to the names and the thank-yous when more priorities were thrown your way? (Civility may go out the window under stress.)
- What happened when you threw the object at somebody before saying their name or without saying their name? (They usually drop it or are not ready for it. We need to let people know when we are sending things their way so they can better prepare for handling it.)
- What happened if the ball was dropped? Did somebody else pick it up? Did the ball sit in the middle of the circle with team members ignoring it – or was it addressed and dealt with?
- Did the volume in the room increase? Do you usually laugh at your mistakes or have a sense of humor about a stressful situation?
- How did you handle all those priorities flying at you at once?
- What happened with the ball of yarn? (It unravels.) Do things sometimes get unraveled as they go along?
- How else can you compare this activity to your workplace or home life?

Contributed by Gail Howerton

23. Just Plane Parts

Objective
> To demonstrate how we are all parts of a larger system

Team Size
> 6 or more people

Time Required
> 10 to 15 minutes, depending on team size

Materials
> ❑ Easel chart
> ❑ Marking pen

Physical Setting
> A space large enough for each team member to see the others and the easel

Process
> Begin with a picture of the major product your company produces or contributes to. Some manufacturing examples might be a plane, a train and a bulldozer. For a service industry, draw a picture of the major product your company services or a picture of the location. Keep the picture simple.

> Introduce the activity as a way to see how we are all parts of whole. "We begin with a picture of our product, and we all add value to that product. Each of us can relate to a part of that product, or as a contributor to the final product. [If you like, give some examples.] So please come up to the chart and draw your 'part' and explain to the team (1) what the part is and (2) why you identify with that part. We have lots of colored markers up here – and don't worry about your artistic ability...you can explain your drawing to us!"

> The team will struggle with your assignment, but let them struggle. You want them to creatively express their roles and their contributions to the team.

47

Debrief and Summarize

After all have had a chance to participate and shared their part, debrief the activity:

- What do you think of your (product)?
- What do you think about your roles on the team?

Be sure each person has a basic understanding of his or her role. Have the team discuss roles if still unclear about how they relate to the overall mission.

24. Map It!

Objective

To creatively demonstrate the geographic diversity and similarities of the team

Team Size

5 to 20 people

Time Required

5 to 20 minutes, depending on team size

Materials

- ❑ Plastic coated 3'x5' geographic map (of the U.S. or the World, depending on the makeup of the team)
- ❑ Removable colored dots

Physical Setting

A space large enough for each team member to see the others and the easel

Process

Before your team assembles, ask each team member to place a small, colored dot on the places they have lived.

Ask each team member to give a quick "tour" for the team, where they have lived and what they were doing at each location. Also ask each team member to share something they remember from their youth (the first dot on the map!).

Debrief and Summarize

After all have had a chance to participate, debrief the activity:

- ♦ What do you think about the activity?
- ♦ What are some of the things we have in common?
- ♦ What are some of the differences between team members?
- ♦ How can these commonalities and differences affect our team work?

Inspired by Steve Holcomb

49

For more team energizers, go to:
www.QPCteam.com

25. Odyssey of the Mind

Objective

To ask team members to think beyond the conventional – to think creatively

Team Size

5 to 25 people

Time Required

5 to 20 minutes, depending on team size

Materials

- ❑ Four to five various interesting household objects, such as an extension cord, unique cooking utensils, etc.

Physical Setting

A space large enough for team members to see each other

Process

Introduce this activity as a way to challenge our creativity, similar to the "Odyssey of the Mind." Ask if anyone is aware of the school program called "Odyssey of the Mind." If no one volunteers, share the origins and purpose:

Sponsored by NASA, Odyssey of the Mind is a school program designed to foster creative thinking and problem-solving skills among students from kindergarten through college. Students solve problems with a variety of different tools. By encouraging children to solve problems in a creative and unique way, students learn lifelong skills such as working with others as a team, evaluating ideas, making decisions and creating solutions while developing self-confidence from their experiences. (For more information, check out www.odysseyofthemind.com)

Now that the team knows what Odyssey of the Mind is all about, encourage the team to think differently about the first object you have in your hand. For example, take an extension cord and wrap it up. It could be an extension cord (traditional thinking) or it could be a whip to beat eggs. Or it could be a lasso.

Tell the team to pass "whatever this is" around the room, and ask each to share what it could be. (Make it okay to pass if they don't have an idea to share quickly. Otherwise, you can get bogged down.)

Hand the extension cord to the next person and ask them to think creatively and ask, "What could this be?"

When the extension cord has been passed to all team members, introduce one or two other objects.

Debrief and Summarize

After all have had a chance to participate, debrief the activity:

- What inspired your creativity?
- What made it difficult to be creative?
- What can we do to encourage creativity on our team?

Inspired by Sally Holloway

26. QTIP

Objective

To provide a quick reminder that "they" aren't out to get us.

Team Size

Any

Time Required

5 minutes

Materials

- ❑ A Q-tip® for each team member

Physical Setting

A space large enough for team members to see each other

Process

As your team walks in, hand them a Q-tip® or place one at each seat. You'll see a few raised eyebrows and hear a few comments about the Q-tip®. Just nod your head knowingly and smile until you are ready for your "icebreaker."

Pick up your Q-tip® and ask if anyone knows what "this" is and what it does.

You'll hear the standard responses, e.g., "to clean your ears." Challenge the team to be more creative...and enjoy the responses!

After all have had a turn, suggest their Q-tip® is a reminder to "**Q**uit **T**aking **I**t **P**ersonally." (Don't worry, some will "get it" immediately...others will need some prompting!)

Debrief and Summarize

With Q-tip® in hand, ask the team what "Quit Taking It Personally" means to them.

- ♦ How can we use or adapt this concept within our team?
- ♦ How might we, as a team, help each other when we take something personally?

Inspired by Linda Thompson who was inspired by Timothy J. O'Brien, Director, Insitute for Stress Management at www.hyperstress.com

For more team energizers, go to:
www.QPCteam.com

27. Quick Vote

Objective

A variation of a rank order vote – a method to vote a long, brainstormed list into a shorter, prioritized list

Team Size

Any

Time Required

10 minutes

Materials

- ❑ A brainstormed list written on easel paper
- ❑ Three different-colored removable dots for each team member

Physical Setting

A space large enough for team members to see each other and the easel

Process

After brainstorming a list on easel paper, ensure that the team members understand what each item means. Combine like items if necessary.

Then give each team member three removable dots, each a different color. For example, give each team member a blue, green and red dot. Explain to the team members that they can vote on the top three items off the brainstorm list. Give the priority of each dot: "Blue is your first choice, green is your second choice, and red is your third choice." Encourage them to write #1, #2 and #3 on the dots, just to make sure they don't get confused.

Ask the team members to silently note how they will vote. Then demonstrate how they should vote by placing the dots in a line next to the brainstormed item.

Ask the team members to come up to the chart and place their dots on the items.

Debrief and Summarize

After all have voted, you now have a brilliant display – typically the "top vote-getter" will pop right out. If there appears to be a tie, the team can easily see how many voted that particular item as #1, #2, or #3 – or – a weighted vote can be tallied. (Note: When counting a weighted vote, the #1 item gets three votes, the #2 item gets 2 votes, and the #3 item gets 1 vote.)

Compare the number of people who voted for the item (the number of dots) versus the weighted vote (the importance each team member placed on that item).

28. Rainbow Connections

Objective

To demonstrate how much we have in common with each other

Team Size

6 to 24 people

Time Required

15 minutes

Materials

☐ Several 9′ long crepe paper streamers or lengths of yarn in several different colors

Physical Setting

A space large enough for the team to stand in a circle

Process

Pair up with a person you don't know very well or don't work with regularly.

Interview each other and discover three things you have in common.

Form a circle with the partners being approximately across from each other. Place a box or basket in the center containing an assortment of nine-foot-long crepe paper streamers or lengths of yarn.

Take a streamer or ball of yarn from the basket, hold one end and hand the other end to your partner. Introduce your partner to the entire group, stating one of the commonalties that you share.

When anyone else hears a comment that they too can identify with, they should say "I can connect with you on that, too" and grab onto the streamer or yarn. Several members of the group may "connect" at the same time, and all will share the streamer to make "connections."

Remind the team to be careful to avoid tearing the paper streamer!

Continue partner introductions and "connecting" until everyone has participated.

Debrief and Summarize

After all have had a chance to participate, debrief the activity:

♦ What do you think about the activity?
♦ What are some of the things we have in common?
♦ What are some of the differences between team members?
♦ How can these commonalities and differences affect our teamwork?

Inspired by Joanne R. Zukowski

29. Read All About It!

Objective

To discover perspectives of each other or our organization

Team Size

Any

Time Required

10 to 15 minutes, depending on team size

Materials

☐ A piece of paper for each team member

Physical Setting

A space large enough for team members to see others and be able to write on a flat surface

Process

Ask each team member to write his or her name on an individual piece of paper. Place the slips into a container.

Have each team member draw out a name (but not their own name!).

Ask each team member to write a newspaper headline describing where that person is after a defined number of years (e.g. three, five or ten years). After the headline, ask them to write a lead paragraph. Give them ten minutes.

Ask each team member to read the headline and lead paragraph to the rest of the team.

Debrief and Summarize

When everyone has read the headlines, debrief the activity:

♦ What did you like most about this activity?
♦ What did you learn about each other?

Variation

To help teams develop vision statements, try this variation:

Break the group into teams.

Have each team write a headline and lead paragraph describing their organization in a defined number of years.

Each team spokesperson introduces their team members and then reads the headline and paragraph.

On an easel chart, capture any recurring themes from the teams.

30. Red Dot, Blue Dot

Objective

To visually allow a team to quickly identify the highest and lowest priorities

Team Size

Any

Time Required

10 minutes

Materials

- ❑ A brainstorm list written on easel charts with a 12   left and right margin
- ❑ Ten red dots and ten blue dots for each team member

Physical Setting

A space large enough for team members to see each other and the easel

Process

Introduce this activity as a way to quickly prioritize a list of items.

Give each team member ten red dots and ten blue dots. *(Note: If the brainstorm list has less than thirty items, divide the number of items by three, and that equals the number of dots).*

Tell the team members to identify where they will place their dots: Red dots go next to items they feel "real hot" about – they are a high priority. Blue dots go next to items they feel are low priorities. Announce whether you want to allow the team members to place multiple dots on one item, or only one dot per item. (Note: if you want a forced distribution, allow only one dot per item. If you want the strength of the items to come out, then allow multiple dots).

Tell the team members to stand up and place the dots on the easelcharts. The red dots go on the left margin of the item, the blue dots go on the right margin.

Debrief and Summarize

After all have had a chance to place the dots on the chart, stand back and see what the highest priorities are.

- What does this information tell us?
- What's a high priority, low priority or no priority?
- Where's the controversy?
- Are there any "pet" issues of one or two team members?

31. Save Everybody!

Objective
> To demonstrate the importance of clearly defining a problem and creatively solving it

Team Size
> 6 or more people

Time Required
> 20 minutes

Materials
> ❑ Titanic model (optional)
> ❑ Iceberg model (optional)

Physical Setting
> A space large enough for the team to separate into smaller groups

Process
> Since most people are familiar with the tragic sinking of the Titanic, start this activity with a graphic of the Titanic, a video clip from the movie where the Titanic collides with the iceberg, or interesting Titanic factoids.

> Describe the problem: Your ship, the USS ****** (think of a great shipboard name) has just collided with an iceberg out in the North Atlantic. The engines are still running, but will stop after an unknown period of time. The ship will sink in two hours, and the ship's officers know this. Unfortunately, the nearest rescue ship is four hours away. There are enough seats in the lifeboats for 1178 people, and there are 2224 on board. In the North Atlantic, a person in the water can live approximately four minutes. Your objective is to 'Save Everybody.'"

> Separate the group into three teams to search for solutions in the following areas:

> - ◆ Upper decks, weather decks, pilot house.
> - ◆ Cabins, dining areas, saloons, gymnasium.
> - ◆ Engine room, machine shops and cargo spaces.

> "You have ten minutes to develop solutions to 'save everybody.' After ten minutes, your team spokesperson will report out your solutions."

> Before reporting out, lead a discussion of what "Save Everybody" really means while capturing the definitions on an easel chart. Hopefully, every team has realized that the problem definition was poor and that a much more solvable problem is something like "keep everyone dry and warm for two more hours until help arrives." Some teams will settle for a self-limiting outcome such as "save as many as we have lifeboat seats for."

Teams report out their solutions, which are discussed by the full group. One team always comes up with the breakthrough idea of putting people on an iceberg using the lifeboats as ferries. Sometimes teams maneuver the ship as long as they have power, either toward the rescue ship or toward the iceberg. Other times, they don't even think of it.

Debrief and Summarize

From your specific observations as well as the discussion, summarize the key learnings from this activity:

- Problem definition affects and may even limit possible outcomes.
- The team had to think "out of the box" and face apparent contradictions (the thing that sank us as the solution to the problem).
- Although the problem was vague, most solutions were, in fact, solving a specific problem.

Reprinted with permission from "Titanic TRIZ: A Universal Case Study" Proceedings of TRIZCON 2000. www.triz-journal.com

32. Soda Can Carry

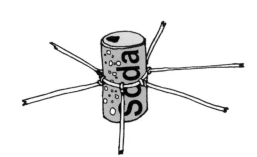

Objective
An exercise to demonstrate the importance of teamwork

Team Size
Groups of 4 to 8 people

Time Required
30 minutes

Materials
For each team:
- One full soda can
- Four pencils
- Two thick rubber bands (strong enough to go around can and be lifted)
- Fifteen-inch piece of string for each person
- Prepared easel paper or whiteboard to "score" the activity

Physical Setting
A space large enough to break the team into smaller groups as well as long enough to carry the soda can from one side of the room to another. Clearly mark point A and point B (with masking tape on the floor)

Process
Introduce this activity as a way to demonstrate the importance of teamwork.

Divide the group into teams of four to eight people. Hand out the materials for each team and give them the task: To carry the soda can (or other soda can) from one side of the room to the other side using the following rules:

- ◆ Each team that successfully carries the soda can from one side of the room to the other side earns 200 points.
- ◆ The soda can is contaminated; therefore no one can come within six inches of the can. If they do, then the team will be fined 10 points for each violation.
- ◆ You cannot upset or turn the can upside down at any time during the exercise. If it is, then the team will be fined 20 points for each violation.
- ◆ You cannot use any other materials than those provided to complete the task. If you do, then the team will be fined 30 points for each violation.
- ◆ Finally, every member of the team must be involved in the carry.

If possible, provide a "starting and finish line" by putting tape on the floor or providing visual points of reference.

Ask if there are any questions and clarify if necessary. Let them know this is not a timed task (no extra points for speed), but you will stop the activity in 20 minutes.

Debrief and Summarize

After all have successfully carried their soda cans to the finish line, debrief the activity:

- What did you like most about this activity?
- What made the team successful?
- How did individual team members help each other?
- How did you make decisions?
- What would you have done differently?
- What did you learn from this activity?
- How might you apply these lessons to our team's work?

Variation

Perform this activity in two rounds:

- Round One: identify one person per group as the "team leader" and the rest are "team members." Have the team leader "direct" all the activities. (Even more fun, blindfold all the team members!)
- Round Two: Allow the team to fully participate in solving the problem.

33. The Sound of Music

Objective
　　To reconnect with team energy

Team Size
　　Any

Time Required
　　5 to 15 minutes, depending on team size

Materials
　　❑ Some of your favorite tunes
　　❑ CD or cassette player

Physical Setting
　　A space large enough for the team to see each other

Process
　　Songs signify events. Think of television theme songs, advertising jingles, college football fight songs, and love songs that couples adopt as "our song." We play "Pomp and Circumstance" at graduations, "Ave Maria" at weddings, and "We are the Champions" at sporting events.

　　Most people have a connection with music, whether it's contemporary music, oldies, pop, classical, country, jazz, R&B, opera – you get the idea!

　　Frank Pacetta suggests, "Music is pure emotion. It has the capacity to form an almost chemical bond with whatever other stray molecules of emotion that are whirring around to form unforgettable and powerful combinations that heighten energy and excitement."

　　Try this activity to discover the music that energizes your team:

　　Ask the team to list their top five (or ten) favorite songs. Then ask them to think back to a moment connected with each piece of music. Chances are, they will rediscover "emotional blasts from the past."

　　Ask each team member to share the list of five (or ten), pick a tune and share the memory.

Kristin's Top Five Songs

The Sound of Music—Julie Andrews
Son of a Sailor—Jimmy Buffet
I Don't Want to Live Without You—Foreigner
House at Pooh Corner—Kenny Loggins
Funny Girl—Barbara Streisand

Debrief and Summarize

After the team has shared its musical moments, ask:

- ♦ Where else in our lives do we use music to inspire and energize?
- ♦ How can we use the emotional energy of music in our team?
- ♦ How can we use music to lighten our load and enjoy our work?
- ♦ What is your team's theme song? When will you play it?

Check out our Extraordinary Team CD, full of music to celebrate team work. Donna's favorite is an adaptation of Jana Stanfield's "We've Started a Conversation." We think you'll like it!

Adapted from Frank Pacetta's book: Stop Whining – and Start Winning

34. Streamline the Process

Objective

To demonstrate the issues associated with improving a process

Team Size

10 to 20 people or groups of 10 to 20 people

Time Required

20 to 30 minutes

Materials

- ❑ A ball (in a pinch, roll up newspaper and wrap tape all over it!)
- ❑ Easel chart
- ❑ Two colored marking pens
- ❑ Stopwatch or watch with second hand
- ❑ Two additional balls (optional)

Physical Setting

A space large enough for the team to stand in a circle and throw a ball around

Process

Introduce this activity as a way to demonstrate the issues around improving a process. Ask the team members to stand up and gather around in a circle.

Explain to the team members that they are employees of the XYZ Company, and they produce a product/service. The ball you are holding is the product/service. The competition is fierce in this business. You have loyal customers, but there is tremendous pressure on your customers to look for top quality and competitive prices. They have come to you and asked you to improve the quality (fewer defects, quicker delivery, lower costs).

Ask all of them to put themselves in the CEO's shoes. Ask the team, "What are you going to do?" The conversation will go off in all different directions, touching all sorts of solutions and improvements. After they have had time to talk, make the point that they are all talking about improvements *when they don't even know what the production process looks like!*

Emphasize to the team that before you can begin improving the process, you must first understand it. And the process starts here, at the warehouse and hand the ball to a team member. Then ask the "warehouse" to throw the ball across the circle to another team member. (Don't forget to call their name before you throw it!) Continue to pass the ball until all team members have touched the ball ONCE.

Take the ball and explain that they have now defined their process. We start with the warehouse and then each person adds value by touching the ball. (Note: you may introduce the concept of an internal customer – that everyone is a supplier and customer in the value chain.)

Give the ball to the warehouse and ask him or her to repeat the process – using the same order. Reinforce that you add value to the process by touching the ball in the same sequence. Tell them that you are going to time how long it takes for the team to complete the process.

After they have passed the ball, post the time on a trend chart labeled "cycle time and defects." Chart the cycle time in one marker color, and chart the "defects" – the ball being dropped – in another color marker. (You may also note the importance of having a baseline time. Without a baseline, you have no reference point for monitoring variation and improvements.)

Depending on how well they completed the first production run, you may want to have them do it again.

"Now that you understand the process, let's try to improve the process." Give them two minutes to identify what they are going to do to improve their process by fifty percent. At the end of two minutes, conduct another production run them, and post the cycle time and defects.

Congratulate them on their performance. They probably hit the target by realigning the people to the work flow.

Ask the team how they went about improving the process. Typically, the team throws out all kinds of ideas and settles on one idea such as rearranging themselves. Make the point that continuous incremental improvement requires that they first identify the root cause(s) of the problem (too much time spent in passing the ball across the room) and then develop a strategy to improve. Also note that if you implement too many strategies for improvement at the same time, they will never really know which change is responsible for the results (better or worse).

Tell them that the company down the street can do it even faster. Give them another two minutes to improve their process by another fifty percent. Reemphasize that everyone adds value to the process by touching the ball in sequence. (Note: reducing staff and/or changing the sequence is not acceptable).

Chart the progress, congratulate them and continue to challenge them to upgrade the process until they have it down to two seconds.

Debrief and Summarize

After you have completed this activity, debrief the process:

- What did you like most about this activity?
- What made the team successful?
- How did individual team members help each other?
- How did you make decisions?
- What would you have done differently?
- What did you learn from this activity?
- How might you apply these lessons to our team's work?

Some typical comments include:

- There is a lot of chaos at first with people brainstorming ideas.
- Pick one idea and see if it works.
- You have to get close to each other.
- Ask for help. Help others.
- Everyone has to be involved and know what's going on.
- Measurements tell us what's important and how we are doing.
- Streamlining can be creative and fun!

Summarize this activity by emphasizing key concepts:

- Continuous, incremental improvement is all about taking one improvement at a time.
- Internal customers – quality is the result of the contributions made at every step of the process (a bad "pass" can lead to problems on the receiver end).
- Complexity – all those additional steps that provide opportunities for error, slow down the process, and add no value to the product/service. (Like calling out each person's name before they pass the ball. It was a safety issue earlier, but now they have a smoother process with less chance for injury).
- Understand the process first. Then improve it.

Variation

After the first production run, all subsequent production runs will include *three* balls. Emphasize that as long as the production run includes all three balls being touched by everyone in sequence, they have met the basic rules. (Note: reducing staff and/or changing the sequence is not acceptable.)

For more team energizers, go to:
www.QPCteam.com

36. Tea Time

Objective
> To take time to reconnect as a team

Team Size
> Any

Time Required
> 5 to 15 minutes, depending on team size

Materials
> ❑ Refreshments

Physical Setting
> A space large enough for the group to mingle about

Process
> At a set time each day ("tea time" at QPC Inc. is at three in the afternoon), suggest that the team stop what they are doing and gather around for "tea time." If there aren't any tea drinkers on the team, suggest they grab a soda, water or other drink as the team chitchats about the day's activities.
>
> Spend ten to fifteen minutes informally sharing what's up. Just knowing that there is time to "connect" on a personal level makes the team more productive. Ask team members to save their stories and socializing for tea time. They can use that time to let each other know what's going on or what to expect from the future.

Inspired by our Extraordinary Team, Neicy Woody and Donna Lantz

For more team energizers, go to:
www.QPCteam.com

37. Team Process Puzzle

Objective
To demonstrate the team process of generating ideas, organizing them, building a consensus to selection, and taking action

Team Size
Groups of 3 people

Time Required
20 minutes

Materials
- ❑ A small, easy-to-assemble jigsaw puzzle for each team (no more than thirty pieces)
- ❑ Paper and pencil/pen for recording observations
- ❑ Large Post-it® notes
- ❑ Black marking pen
- ❑ Easel chart or whiteboard to post ideas

Physical Setting
A space with table(s) for each group to assemble a small jigsaw puzzle

Process
Tell the group it will be modeling a typical team process of generating information, organizing that information so the team can select one or more options to act on.

Ask people to group themselves into teams of three; two people will be putting the puzzle together while the third person will observe the process.

Hand out one puzzle to each team. Tell the teams "the goal is to assemble the puzzle and for the process observer to record how the teams put the puzzle together. For example, the first step is to open the box." Encourage the observers to take notes and assure the teams that this is NOT a competition.

Allow the teams to complete the puzzle. Cheer when each team completes the puzzle.

When all teams have completed the puzzles, debrief the activity by asking the process observers, "How did your teams put the puzzle together from the starting point of opening up the box to when the puzzle was completed?" (While you are giving these directions, write "open box" at the top of the easel chart and "puzzle complete" at the bottom of the easel chart.)

Ask for one idea from each observer, and with a large marker, legibly write each idea on a large Post-it® note. Place the Post-it® notes on the easel chart, with all the "generation" ideas toward the top, "organization" ideas toward the middle, "decisions" in the lower half and "take action" on the bottom. Place communication issues along the side of the easel chart. Depending on the level of detail and number of teams, the group will identify ten to fifteen steps in the process.

(Note: This models the "generation" of information – specifically the steps to assemble a jigsaw puzzle. By placing the Post-it® notes in pre-determined categories, you are "organizing" the information into categories, as well as into a flowchart.)

Congratulate the teams on "generating" many steps to assemble a jigsaw puzzle, which you have posted on the easel chart. Point out the similarities to "brainstorming" – which is the primary tool used to generate information.

Reinforce the analogy that teams generate ideas, organize them, select what needs to be done and then take action – just like teams put a puzzle together.

Using the team's Post-it® notes, compare the notes to the process that teams use to:

Generate
- Look at/open the box – Define what you are brainstorming.
- Dump the pieces out – Brainstorm/generate ideas.
- Turn the pieces over – Make sure everyone understands what was said or meant.

Organize
- Find the corners – Organize or sort the ideas by categories.
- Group same colors/animals/puzzle subject together – Organize or sort the ideas by categories.

Decide
- Agree to focus on the frame – Decide what to do/how to proceed.
- Agree that one person will assemble one part of the puzzle together and the other person will assemble another part together – Decide roles.

Act
- Put puzzle together – Take action.
- Clap hands – Celebrate success!

Debrief and Summarize
Point out the different ways the teams organized their pieces (by color, by picture objects, corners and sides). Draw the parallel that many teams organize the information differently, depending on the subject. They might make a flowchart from one point to another, prioritize it by importance, sort it into categories, place it on a timeline, etc.

Point out the subtle ways that teams are always making small decisions – often times without verifying that the team has made a decision! Ask the group how they made decisions while putting the puzzle together – relying on the "puzzle expert," the loudest voice, a majority vote, or a consensus. Discuss the different ways teams make decisions and quickly move into action.

Finally, debrief the communication flow – checking with each other, referring to the goal (the picture of the completed puzzle on the box), as well as roadblocks to effective team communication.

From your specific observations as well as the discussion, summarize the key learnings from this activity.

For more team energizers, go to:
www.QPCteam.com

38. Team Openers

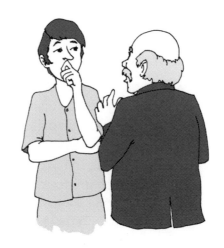

Objective

To encourage team members to come together and "form" faster and to allow team members to "open" up

Team Size

Any

Time Required

5 to 10 minutes, depending on team size

Materials

❑   A good, well-thought-out question

Physical Setting

A space large enough for each team member to see and hear each other

Process

When teams are first forming, ask each team member to complete *one* of the following statements. Assure team members that they can pass if they want as well as ask questions for clarity (not to challenge):

- ♦ The purpose of this team is to...
- ♦ From this team experience, I want to gain/get...
- ♦ To help this team succeed, I bring these strengths to the team:...
- ♦ One thing that makes me a good team player is...
- ♦ I am most proud of...
- ♦ My most significant accomplishment is...
- ♦ My main concern about being on this team is...
- ♦ The expertise I bring to this team is...
- ♦ The one thing that frustrates me the most about working in teams is...
- ♦ In order to achieve our goal, I think the potential hurdles we may face are...

Capture the answers on an easel chart.

Debrief and Summarize

When all have had an opportunity to share, debrief the lists:

- ♦ Are there any common themes?
- ♦ How does this affect our team's work?
- ♦ Is there some action we need to take?

Variations

Once the team has formed, you may want to branch out into other types of "fill-in-the-blank" statements and questions that allow team members to get to know each other better:

- What's your favorite sports team and why?
- What's your favorite vacation spot and why?
- What's your favorite book and why?
- What's your favorite movie and why?
- Who made the biggest impact on you as you were growing up?
- Tell us about your first job and something you learned there that is still useful today.
- Describe a "Great Day" in your life (i.e., a memorable day from any stage of your life that you remember as one of the great days).

39. Test for Consensus: A Straw Poll

Objective

To allow the team to see what it thinks of a decision, without actually agreeing on the final outcome

Team Size

Any

Time Required

10 minutes

Materials Required

- ❑ A prepared easel chart with "5L" scale

Loathe   Lament   Live   Like   Love

- ❑ One removable colored dot for each team member

Physical Setting

A space large enough for team members to see each other and the easel

Process

When aiming for consensus, take a "straw poll" of the team's energy and commitment to a specific outcome using this fun and simple tool.

First, ensure a complete understanding of the straw poll issue. Clarify any lingering questions the team may have.

Then have each person take one colored dot. (Note: you may "stratify" the team by giving different colored dots to distinct groups.)

Draw the "5L" scale on the easelchart. Walk through the definitions of each "L" and ask team members to silently vote on what they think of the solution:

- ♦ "You **loathe** it or hate it.
- ♦ You will **lament** it and moan about it in the parking lot.
- ♦ You can **live** with it.
- ♦ You **like** it.
- ♦ You really **love** it."

Ask the team members to place their colored dot on the item, so that they are building a bar chart. After all have placed their dots on the easelchart, step back and evaluate.

Debrief and Summarize

Based on the results of the straw poll, see if the team agrees there is consensus. Consensus is that all votes are at least a "live with" or better.

In the event there are votes that are "loathe," "lament," or just a few "live with," ask the team why someone voted that way. Be careful not to pick on a specific person, but get the team's feedback on why there isn't consensus.

Integrate the new feedback and build a better solution.

40. Tinker Toys®

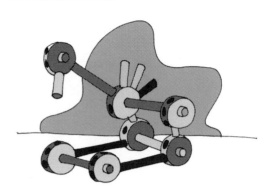

Objective
To observe how easily communication can break down

Team Size
Two groups of 4 to 8 people

Time Required
30 minutes

Materials
❑   Two sets of Tinker Toys®

Physical Setting
Two rooms (or one room with a physical divider)

Process
Divide into two groups. Instruct each group to quickly build a Tinker Toy® structure, without letting the other group see the structure.

Send one representative from each group to the other group. The representative will instruct the other group on how to replicate the structure, based *solely* on verbal description.

Debrief and Summarize
When finished, let the two groups observe the other's structure. From your specific observations as well as the discussion, debrief the activity:

- ♦   How did the group representative communicate with the other group?
- ♦   What helped the communication?
- ♦   What got in the way of the communication?
- ♦   What frustrations did the groups encounter?
- ♦   What did you learn from this activity?
- ♦   How might we apply these lessons to our team's work?

Variation
Conduct three rounds:

Round One – the representative gives verbal description, but the group may not ask any questions.

Round Two – the representative gives verbal description and the group may ask questions.

Round Three – the representative gives verbal description and may make suggestions.

For more team energizers, go to:
www.QPCteam.com

41. To Build a Bridge

Objective

To develop cooperation among team members and to gain problem-solving experience

Team Size

Groups of 4 to 8 people

Time Required

10 to 15 minutes

Materials

- ❑ One entire issue of a newspaper per group
- ❑ Masking tape
- ❑ Bowl of candy (disposable bowls work really well!)

Physical Setting

A space large enough for the team to separate into smaller groups

Process

Introduce the purpose of the exercise: to experience the importance of paying attention to work processes and team relationships, as well as results.

Explain the desired results of the exercise: the state or local transportation department needs a new bridge design and the group has been assigned the task. The available materials are newspaper and masking tape.

The criteria for building a successful bridge are to: (1) be able to stand up on its own, (2) be wide enough at the base for the bowl of candy to slide through (like a boat going under a bridge); and (3) be strong enough to support the weight of the bowl of candy (like a car traveling over the bridge).

Ask if there are any questions and if they all understand the process – then let 'em go!

When a group finishes the bridge, check for success and then celebrate by clapping and allowing the team to eat the candy!

Debrief and Summarize

After the teams have successfully constructed the bridges, debrief the activity:

- What did you like most about this activity?
- What made the team successful?
- What process, if any, did you use to "design" the bridge?
- Who emerged as the group leader(s)? What characteristics did the leader(s) display?
- Did everyone participate? If not, why not?
- Describe the group dynamic.
- How did individual team members help each other?
- How did you make decisions?
- What would you have done differently?
- What did you learn from this activity?
- How might you apply these lessons to our team's work?

Contributed by Kay Freidinger

42. To Build a Tower

Objective
To demonstrate the value of planning and teamwork

Team Size
Groups of 4 to 10 people

Time Required
30 minutes

Materials
- ❑ Prepared easel paper or whiteboard with the criteria for success
- ❑ One sheet of easel chart paper for each group
- ❑ For each group, one large zipper plastic bag with all of the below materials:
  - o One pair of scissors
  - o Three paper cups
  - o Three paper plates
  - o One marking pens
  - o One roll of masking tape
  - o Four index cards (5"x7")
  - o Four index cards (3"x5")
  - o Four plastic coffee stirrers

Physical Setting
A space large enough for the team to separate into smaller groups

Process
Introduce the purpose of the exercise: to experience the importance of paying attention to work processes and team relationships, as well as results.

Explain the desired results of the exercise: to build a free-standing tower using only the materials provided.

The ground rules are as follows: You will have fifteen minutes to plan and seven minutes to build the tower. You cannot touch the materials during the fifteen minutes of planning.

The criteria for success are: (1) the tower is free-standing (not attached to the floor, walls, etc.); (2) the tower must be at least five feet tall; and (3) the tower must be able to survive a moderate wind.

For an added bit of fun, ask for the "measurers" – someone who knows what "free standing" is; someone who is at least five feet tall, and someone who can blow a moderate wind! You will then use these folks to verify the success of each tower.

Ask if there are any questions and if they all understand the process – then let 'em go!

After fifteen minutes, tell the teams they have seven minutes to build.

After seven minutes, gather all around the center of the room, bringing the towers!

Have each measurer check each tower. (Note: On average, only half the towers succeed. For those groups who get depressed over not "winning," you can have a great conversation about competition and the impact of time).

Debrief and Summarize
After all the towers have been judged, debrief the activity:

- What did you like most about this activity?
- What made the team successful?
- What process, if any, did you use to "design" the tower?
- Who emerged as the group leader(s)? What characteristics did the leader(s) display?
- Did everyone participate? If not, why not?
- Describe the group dynamic.
- How did individual team members help each other?
- How did you make decisions?
- What would you have done differently?
- What did you learn from this activity?
- How might you apply these lessons to our team's work?

Variation
Halfway through the planning phase (about seven minutes), quietly remove one team member from each team and replace him or her with someone from one of the other teams. This wil give the teams a chance to work the relationship issue, trying to deal with the loss of a valued member as well as decide how to quickly bring the new person on board. Some will do well here, others may choose to ignore the new person.

Inspired by Jeff Anthony

43. To Build a Tower, Version Two

Objective

To demonstrate the value of teamwork

Team Size

Groups of 3 to 6 people

Time Required

20 to 25 minutes, depending on team size

Materials

- ❑ One box of straight straws (not flexible) for each group
- ❑ Paper clips that fit snugly into the straws

Physical Setting

A space large enough for the team to separate into smaller groups

Process

Introduce the purpose of the exercise: to demonstrate the value of teamwork.

Explain the desired results of the exercise: to build a free-standing tower using only the materials provided in fifteen minutes.

The criteria for success are: (1) the tower is free-standing (not attached to the floor, walls, etc.); (2) the tower must be at least five feet tall; and (3) the tower must be able to survive a moderate wind.

For an added bit of fun, ask for the "measurers" – someone who knows what "free standing" is; someone who is at least five feet tall, and someone who can blow a moderate wind! You will then use these folks to verify the success of each tower.

Ask if there are any questions and if they all understand the process – then let 'em go!

After fifteen minutes, ask the groups to gather all around the center of the room, bringing the towers!

Have each measurer check each tower. Typically, most of the towers succeed.

Debrief and Summarize
Debrief what worked and what the teams could have done better, and tie it into the team learning points.

- What did you like most about this activity?
- What made the team successful?
- What process, if any, did you use to "design" the tower?
- Who emerged as the group leader(s)? What characteristics did the leader(s) display?
- Did everyone participate? If not, why not?
- Describe the group dynamic.
- How did individual team members help each other?
- How did you make decisions?
- What would you have done differently?
- What did you learn from this activity?
- How might you apply these lessons to our team's work?

Variation
Change the criteria for success to include a competitive edge, (e.g., tallest, strongest, most creative, most functional, etc.).

44. Tug of War

Objective

To creatively demonstrate the use of the of the force-field analysis "tool"

Team Size

8 people or more

Time Required

10 minutes

Materials

- ❑ Long rope with red tape in middle
- ❑ Pen

Physical Setting

A space large enough for eight people to have a tug of war in front of the team

Process

Explain to the team that there are a lot of forces "driving" the team to move in a new direction. Ask for four volunteers to line up on one side of you.

Explain to the team that there are a lot of forces "restraining" or keeping the team from moving in a new direction. Ask for four more volunteers to line up on the other side of you.

Explain to the team that whenever you are trying to change something, there are driving forces and restraining forces – much like a tug of war. Then let the teams pull on each side, trying to "win."

Debrief and Summarize

From this discussion, debrief the activity:

- So what happened?
- Who won? (Typically, no one really wins...)
- Does this happen when we try to institute a change?
- What are some of the reasons for this? (It's important to understand *where* people are coming from and *why* they are pulling so hard.)
- Is there a "show-stopper" in the crowd? (Sometimes, there's a legal, safety or ethical reason why we can't move forward.)
- How might we be able to ensure we can move in the new direction?
  - Bolster the strengths (add people, muscle, etc.).
  - Mitigate the restraining forces (take away people, muscle, etc.).

Inspired by Beth Scolton

45. Walking Our Talk

Objective

To help the team to form a way of working with each other that is consistent with the way clients/patients/customers are treated by their organization

Team Size

Groups of 8 to 10 people

Time Required

10 to 15 minutes, depending on team size

Materials

- ❑ Easel chart or whiteboard
- ❑ Marking pens

Physical Setting

A space large enough for team members to see each other and the easel

Process

Ask the group to describe how someone seeking services or care should expect to be treated when coming to its organization. If the size of the group is twenty or less, it can be done together. If the group is larger than twenty, form groups of eight to ten and ask someone to record. If there are break-out groups, come together and report. Record the group comments on easel chart.

Ask the team how someone who joins the team should expect to be treated. Write the answers on an easel chart.

When finished brainstorming, discuss differences between the ways a customer/client/patient is treated and how the team is treating one another.

Debrief and Summarize

Discuss how the team can better "walk its talk" by agreeing to work out ways to treat each other as a client/customer/patient would be treated.

Contributed by Carol Weisman

For more team energizers, go to:
www.QPCteam.com

46. The Web We Weave

Objective

To demonstrate the interrelationships and importance of each team member – particularly at the end of the team's work

Team Size

5 or more people

Time Required

10 to 20 minutes, depending on team size

Materials

❑ A ball of yarn

Physical Setting

A space large enough for the team to gather (sit or stand) in a circle

Process

As a way to bring closure to individual contributions to the team's success, ask the team to sit in a circle. Hold a ball of yarn in your hand and begin the process by saying, "We all are important to this team's success. And we couldn't have been successful without your individual contributions. So let's celebrate and thank our teammates. Here's how I suggest we proceed: I'll start by saying I would like to thank (Name) for (accomplishment). (For example, I'd like to thank Larry for staying late one night, when I knew it wasn't convenient, to finish compiling the numbers for the team.)"

Once you have thanked the person, wrap the yarn around your finger, and throw the ball to that person. Then they thank someone else, wrap the yarn around the finger, and throw the ball to the person you thanked, etc.

After several passes, we start to weave a web of interconnectivity and dependence on each team member. (Yes, there is a risk that one or two team members didn't pull their weight...usually the team will make sure they get included somehow, but the message does get sent in a subtle manner that they, in fact, did not pull their weight!)

Continue until the activity appears to slow down, but check with the team first. Once, I was surprised that the team was having such a great time, they wanted to continue for five more minutes!

Debrief and Summarize

At the end, ask the team to look at the web we weave. "We are only as strong as all of us. And then look at what happens when we aren't there to help each other. Please, take the yarn off your finger." The yarn looses its beautiful shape and form!

Or:

Ask one team member to grab as much yarn as they can. See how one person can affect the balance of the team dynamic.

Variation

For new teams, whomever catches the ball has to share a "fact" about themselves – either personal or work-related.

Inspired by Sally Holloway

47. When Shall We Meet Again?

Objective
To demonstrate how teams assess information to make a decision

Team Size
5 or more people

Time Required
15 minutes

Materials
- ❑ Prepared easel chart
- ❑ The following bullets neatly printed on separate index cards
  - ◆ The team agreed that Mondays are a bad time to meet. Everybody's just returning from the weekend and preparing for the work week.
  - ◆ Mary usually takes the minutes.
  - ◆ Many people in the office go bowling on Thursday nights.
  - ◆ The coffee machine is three doors down from the conference room.
  - ◆ The conference room has an oval table with ten chairs around it.
  - ◆ John and Kathy always arrive at work by 6:30 a.m.
  - ◆ There are markers and an easel chart in the conference room.
  - ◆ Sally and Roger have to leave work by 4 p.m.
  - ◆ The team agreed that Fridays are a bad time to meet. Everybody's preparing to leave for the weekend (if they haven't already left).
  - ◆ The company has 211 employees.
  - ◆ Kristin is the team leader.
  - ◆ Treena thinks that team meetings are usually a waste of time.
  - ◆ Ken has been looking forward to the team meeting. He has a very important issue he'd like to raise.
  - ◆ The overhead projector light bulb is burned out.
  - ◆ There isn't a whiteboard in the conference room.
  - ◆ The team leader prepares the agenda and leads the meeting.
  - ◆ Kristin is going to be out of town on Tuesday and Wednesday.
  - ◆ The conference room is booked on Thursday from 8 a.m. to 12 noon.
  - ◆ The conference room is booked on Wednesday from 8 a.m. to 12 noon.

Physical Setting
A space large enough for the team to sit in a circle or U-shape

Process
Invite the group to participate in a team activity that will give them a glimpse into the group dynamic. Tell the group, "The team needs to meet for four hours next week. You have been exchanging emails to determine the best weekday and time to meet. The emails are written on these index cards."

Mix up the cards and give at least one card to each team member. Remind them that their task is to answer the question written on the easel chart: "Given the following information you received by email (on the index cards), when will your team meet (weekday and time) next week?"

Then stand out of the way and watch the team dynamics!

The answer is deceptively simple: The team must meet on Thursday from 12 noon until 4 p.m. The team has agreed it cannot meet on Mondays and Fridays. Kristin has to be at the meeting, and she'll be out of town on Tuesday and Wednesday. The conference room is booked on Thursday from 8 a.m. to 12 noon.

As the team attempts to solve the riddle, you may witness some common traps:

- **No process.** The team just starts shouting out the information they have on the cards, without planning how to handle the task.
- **Process loss.** The team ignores someone who has the answer (or something close to it).
- **Assumptions.** The team begins to make assumptions about the information—what is relevant and what isn't—without any criteria to assess it.
- **A hero emerges.** One person solves the riddle and declares victory, while making his/her teammates feel left out or stupid.
- **Poor communication skills.** Talking over each other, interrupting, dominating the conversation.
- **Agonize about the irrelevant.** Just in case they miss something, the team goes over each piece of information.
- **Paranoia sets in.** Could it be a trap? Could it be one of those team activities that "get you" in the end? Is there something the facilitator just isn't telling us?

Eventually, the team figures out it needs structure/process. One person will take the "leadership role," define a process, and facilitate the team to the logical conclusion.

Debrief and Summarize
- What worked well for the team?
- What helped the communication process?
- What frustrations did you encounter?
- What could the team have done better?
- How might we apply these lessons to our team's work?

Variation
If the group is large or you want to add to the confusion, add your own irrelevant information cards!

48. Where Are We Going?

Objective
    To creatively demonstrate the power of a collective vision

Team Size
    Any

Time Required
    5 minutes

Materials
    □ Easel paper
    □ Marking pen

Physical Setting
    A space large enough for the group to mingle about and gather in a circle

Process
    Ask the team members to close their eyes. Ask, "Where are we going? Please point your finger to where you think we are going."

    After everyone has pointed somewhere, ask the team members to open their eyes. Many fingers might be pointed in the same general direction, but there are probably many fingers pointed all over the room.

    Ask, "What would need to happen to have everyone pointing their fingers in the same direction?" Capture the answers on an easel chart.

Debrief and Summarize
    After all have had a chance to participate, debrief the activity:

- ♦ Does the team have a collective vision? Do you know where you are going?
- ♦ What actions are you willing to take to be "in alignment" with the vision?

    Summarize by commenting on the power of a common vision and teams. By sharing the vision with our team members, we can all move toward the same direction.

Variation

If you like, continue this activity by demonstrating the power of communicating a common vision. "I envision that this team needs to go to Los Angeles next Tuesday to deliver a presentation on this team at 10 a.m. to the media about a specific project." Repeat the vision. Let it sink in.

Ask, "What are you thinking? What needs to be done in order to be successful in Los Angeles?" Quickly go around the room and ask what is on the top of their minds (e.g., plane tickets, putting together the presentation, what are we going to do in L.A.? etc.).

Emphasize the point that people are naturally goal seeking, and once given a vision of the future, can figure out how to get there.

49. Win or Lose?

Objective

To provide a structured opportunity for groups to experience competition and opportunities for cooperation and collaboration between functional organizations

Team Size

4 groups of equal size

Time Required

15 to 20 minutes, depending on team size

Materials

- ❑ Prepared easel chart of payoff schedule
- ❑ Prepared easel chart with a table of each division across the top
- ❑ Marking pen

Physical Setting

A space large enough for each group to collaborate

Process

Create four teams of relatively equal size and name them for functional divisions within an organization (e.g., Human Resources, Sales, Marketing, Production).

Instruct the teams that they are divisions within an organization and that their goal is to make money by voting for the organization. Money is made or lost as they vote either "Green" or "Blue" and by their voting pattern in accordance with the following payoff schedule:

4 Green	Lose $100 each
3 Green	Win $100 each
2 Green	Win $200 each
1 Green	Win $300 each
4 Blue	Win $100 each
3 Blue	Lose $100 each
2 Blue	Lose $200 each
1 Blue	Lose $300 each

For example, Sales votes "Blue" and the other three divisions vote "Green." Sales would lose $300, and the other three divisions would win $100. Display the totals on a tally sheet:

Round	Sales	HR	Marketing	Production
1	-$300	$100	$100	$100
2				
total				
3				
total				
4				
total				
5				
total				

Do not elaborate further on these instructions. Repeat them as necessary. At the close of each round, tally each division's dollar balance in that division's column.

Play five rounds according to the following instructions:

Round One – No additional instructions given. Discussions within the group, but not between groups.

Round Two – Same as round one (it takes two basic rounds before they really start to catch on to the game).

Round Three – Each group selects a delegate, and the delegates circulates from group to group, lobbying for the groups to vote a particular way; delegates return to their groups and the vote is taken.

Round Four – Delegates meet together privately and then return to their groups and the vote is taken.

Round Five – Same as rounds one and two; no discussion between groups.

After all five rounds, tally the total amounts earned by each division and then the company's net worth.

Debrief and Summarize

After computing the totals, debrief the activity:

- Is the division amounts and company's net worth positive or negative?
- Who won? Who lost?
- What factors contributed to a sense of competition between the groups?
- What factors fostered cooperation between the groups?
- What factors mask the fact that the company's overall goal is to make money?

Contributed by Merri Hanson

50. You're the Expert!

Objective
To creatively demonstrate the power of teamwork versus an individual's work

Team Size
Groups of 3 people

Time Required
1o minutes

Materials
- ❑ A universally familiar object, such as a telephone, coin, currency, company insignia, etc.
- ❑ Easel chart
- ❑ Paper
- ❑ Pens

Physical Setting
A space large enough for the team to sit in a U-shape or circle

Process
Introduce this activity as a way to demonstrate the power of team work.

Before you get started, make sure the object is not accessible to the team members (e.g., ask everyone to hide the cellular phones).

Ask if there is anyone in the room who uses a telephone. Ask them if they would consider themselves to be a frequent user, or "expert" on using a specific object (such as a telephone)?

Draw the outline of the object (e.g., twelve "buttons") on an easel chart in front of the room. Ask each person to individually fill in the object (e.g., numbers and the letters on the telephone keypad).

After a few minutes, ask the team to break into groups of three to make a group agreement on the specifics of the object (e.g., numbers and letters on the telephone keypad).

While the groups are contemplating the answer, fill in the object (e.g., numbers and letters) on the easel chart, out of sight of the groups.

After the groups are done, expose the easel chart to the team.

Debrief and Summarize

After all have seen the "answer" and compared their work to the "answer," debrief the activity:

- Which did better? The individual or group? (Most of the time, the group has a better answer. Every once in a while, an individual has a better answer – this is called "process loss" where those great ideas were not integrated to the larger team).
- How did the team come up with a better answer? What process did you use?
- How can we replicate this in our team?
- How can we guard against process loss?

Debriefing An Activity

What's the point of doing an team energizer or activity? We all know the answer – to help team members learn in a real-world, hands on way. But have you considered the fact that learning doesn't actually happen during the activity, but during the discussion after the activity is over?

In my experience, the process of debriefing (the official word for this after-the-activity dialogue) is mostly overlooked, usually unplanned, and often poorly executed. What a shame! Ignoring the skills, planning, and practice required by debriefing might just be at the root of much of the criticism leveled at activities during learning sessions. How often have you heard people say – not after one of your sessions of course – "We had fun, but I'm not sure anyone learned anything." Or, "Why do they have us do these things, we've got too much real work to do to waste time on stuff like this." In my research, the reason for the glaring omission of this basic skill became clear. Pick any book on training or facilitation off your bookshelf. Check the index for *debriefing*. If you find a reference at all, it is apt to consist of a paragraph that tells you, "don't forget to do a debriefing," or "conduct a debrief." Not much help if you want to conduct an effective debrief. So here it is; an overview of the ingredients of a successful debriefing and a model to follow. Ignore these pages at your own risk!

To ensure effective debriefing you need three ingredients – time, questions, and silence.

Time. Thiagi (an acknowledged master of learning activities) was quoted as saying that the debriefing should last at least as long as the exercise. You do the math. A 20-minute activity actually needs to be scheduled for 40 minutes. 20 to have the experience and 20 to talk and learn from the experience. A 60-minute simulation requires two hours. You get the point. In our "can't you do this session in a half day rather than two days" world, this is a significant consideration. Master trainers and facilitators know how to make the tough decisions; they'll eliminate an activity rather than short change the time for the debrief of the first exercise.

Questions. The heart of a good debrief is the questions asked. Master facilitators and trainers don't worry if an activity doesn't unfold in the way they planned. They know that by asking the participants a series of well-thought-out questions, quality insights will emerge no matter what the activity outcome. The confidence that I, the facilitator, can help a group find the "a-ha's" necessary for learning no matter what happens, isn't born from arrogance. It comes from hard work – developing a list of great questions at the same time I'm developing the activity. These questions need to cover all the possible outcomes I can imagine as well as crafting a few questions for the outcomes I can't imagine. The debriefing model that follows will help you think through the types of questions you'll need to work on.

Silence. All facilitation is about dialogue and nowhere is dialogue more important than debriefing. How many times have you been overwhelmed by the insight announced to you by someone else? How much more meaningful has an insight been when you discovered it for yourself? It is when participants look at their collective or individual behavior and recognize its impact, that they can learn. Debriefing, when done by a master, often consists of a carefully crafted question followed by a long stretch of silence. Silence provides the space for remembering, thinking, and processing necessary for learning to take place. Silence allows the facilitator or trainer to see the faint glow of mental light bulbs begin to understand. Trying to nurture a meaningful dialogue without understanding the true meaning and use of silence – well it just doesn't work.

In *The Instant Trainer*, a book I wrote with C. Leslie Charles, Leslie shared her model for debriefing. I offer it here as a way to capture the debriefing process as well as an easy way for you to structure your debriefing as you plan your sessions. Leslie's four- step process is called SAGE.

S stands for **SHARE**

The opening step in debriefing consists of a series of questions that ask the participants to reflect upon and report their experiences. These are the WHAT questions. In the Share phase you ask participants to describe what they saw, felt, thought, or observed during the activity. If your activity has put people into smaller groups, don't forget that these subgroups may have had different experiences. They'll need to understand the differences in their experiences in order to move to the next steps. During this stage you, the facilitator or trainer, might have to add a few observations if the group has idealized their experience. Just remember to keep your observations as neutral reporting rather than judgments.

Questions for this phase most often start with *What*.
- What happened in your group?
- What did you think when...?

A stands for **ANALYZE**

This stage starts the reflection that is central to a debriefing. Here you ask participants for their interpretation of what they think happened. People are asked to analyze their experiences and draw personal conclusions as to cause and effect. The primary question in this stage centers on why people reacted as they did. Learners are asked to contrast, compare, infer, explore, and analyze not only what happened, but why. These questions will help you draw out people's perceptions and interpretations of the event that just happened.

Questions for this phase most often start with *Why*.
- Why do you think the group (you) reacted that way?
- Why was that reaction significant?

G stands for **GENERALIZE**

Once your group members have identified and analyzed what happened to them during your structured activity, you now want them to relate their experience to real life. This is the *transfer* phase where an insight gained can be brought back into one's everyday existence. You will ask participants to connect what they just experienced with their world. The primary question is When, as in, "When did you experience a similar situation?" You want people to recognize how their behavior in this simulation or exercise mirrors how they normally behave. By asking your learners to generalize in the classroom how their group experience relates to situations they face each day at work or at home, you have raised their awareness to a new level. Insight, realization, self-reflection, and personal analysis often result in the beginning of permanent behavior or attitude change.

Questions for this phase most often start with *When*.
- When have you had a similar experience in real life?
- When might a situation like this effect your working relationships?

E stands for **EVALUATE**

Once you've conducted this experience, managed the dialogue, and moved through the debriefing process to this point, you need to create the place where participants can think through the behavior changes they need to take to move insight into action. The questions in this stage often begin with How as in, "How are you going to do things differently?" This is the real purpose of debriefing. It cannot happen successfully, however, without the dialogue that occurs during the first three phases.

Questions for this phase most often start with *How*.
- How can this experience help you change they way you work together?
- How will you start that change?

Using the SAGE model will help you effectively debrief your activities. Write down your questions for each phase. Don't get hung up with fitting your questions to the *what, why, when, how* beginnings – they're identified to help you organize your thoughts, not limit your creativity. Recognize and take advantage of the fact that you'll be struck by genius in the moment and a perfect question will appear out of nowhere – just don't rely on divine inspiration – do your homework. Investing time and energy in both thinking about and improving your debriefing skills has a high return on investment for both you and your participants.

Contributed by Chris Clarke-Epstein, CSP

Additional Resources

There are a bazillion books (like this one) on team activities – far too many to list here! The key is to be able to select the perfect activity that strikes the perfect cord with your team. So how do you find that perfect team energizer?

Go to our website, www.qpcteam.com and look for the team energizer search engine. Answer some basic questions, and the search engine will find your answer! You will need to know:

- The subject/type of activity you are looking for
- Whether it is an individual or group activity
- How much time you have on your agenda for the activity
- Whether the activity will be held inside or outside (or it doesn't matter)
- The minimum number of people who will be participating
- The maximum number of people who will be participating

The search engine will comb through all the team activities we have on file, and provide a list of all activities that meet the search criteria, including:

- The name of the activity
- The name of the book and publisher
- The published objectives for the activity
- The page number where you can find that activity

If you already own the book, just look it up! If you don't own the book, you will have the option to purchase that particular book through our website, or continue searching!

We're really excited about this new service we are offering – free of charge to you. We welcome your comments and suggestions, as well as recommended additions to our database.

Happy hunting for that extraordinary team energizer!

Index

Aardvark and Antelope, 1–2
ABC concept, 14
active listening, 3–4, 17
Active Listening, 3–4
activity debriefing, 107-109
affinity diagram, 5–6
Affinity Nametag, 5–6
agenda, 13–14
analysis phase, 108
Analogy method, 9
Anthony, Jeff, 90
appropriateness, vii
Assigning Priority, 7–8
assumptions, 99

Balance, 45–46
Biech, Elaine, 58
BINGO. *see* Cliché Bingo
boundaries, 20
brainstorming, 5, 9–10, 55, 69–71, 78
Brainstorming Variations, 9—10
Break Out Groups, 11–12
Build an Agenda, 13–14
Building an Extraordinary Team,
      15–16
bulletin boards, 31

Caroselli, Marlene, 40
Chain Reaction method, 9
Chain Story, 17
Change!, 19–20
Charles, C. Leslie, 108
cheating, 46
Check in and Check Out, 21
civility, 46
Clarke-Epstein, Chris, 109
Cliché Bingo, 22–24
closure, 21, 97–98
collaboration, 103
collective vision, 101
common ground, 49, 57
communication, 16, 85, 100
competition, 103
Compressed method, 10
conflict management, 16
consensus, 77, 83–85
cooperation, 16, 87, 103–104

counting off, 12
creativity, 17, 51–52

Debriefing, 107-109
decision making, 1, 16, 25–26, 37, 77–
      79, 83–84, 99–100
Decisions, Decisions, 25–26
Deck of Cards, The, 27–30
Deming, W. Edwards, 27–30
dialogue, 108
Dilbert, 24
diversity, 16, 49
dropping the ball, 48
Dube, Brother Richard, 31

Empathetic listening, 4
energy, 67–68
evaluation phase, 109
extraordinary teams, 15

Face the Facts, 31
feedback, 43–44
5L scale, 83
flexibility, vii
Follow the Process, 33–34
force-field analysis tool, 93
forming, 21, 81–82
Freewheel method, 10

Generalization phase, 109
generating ideas, 77
goals, 15, 73
Gordian Knot, 35–36
ground rules, 20
group size. *see* team size

Hanson, Merri, 104
Hats We Wear, The, 37–38
high performance teams, 15
Holcomb, Steve, 30, 49
Holloway, Sally, 26, 52, 98
H-O-M-E-S Is Where the Heart Is,
      39–40
hot topics, 3
"how" questions, 109
Howerton, Gail, 46
HR Handbook, 58

Huddle, The, 41–42
humor, 46

Icebreakers, vii
Idea Quota method, 10
Instant Trainer, 108
internal customers, 69–71
Inversion method, 10
irrelevance, 100
Johari Window, 43–44
Jones, John E., 58
Juggling Priorities, 45–46
Just Plane Parts, 47–48

Keep It Simple method, 10

Lantz, Donna, 75
listening, 16. *see also* active listening

Maintenance roles, 15
Map It!, 49
Martian method, 10
memory, 39–41
Mercier, Larry, 20
mnemonic device, 39
music, 67–68

Odyssey of the Mind, 51–52
organization, 77
Osborne, Alex F., 9
overadjusting, 27

Pacetta, Frank, 68
paranoia, 100
passing, vii
personalizing, 53
Physical characteristics method, 12
planning, 89
preparation, vii
Preselection method, 12
Presorted toys method, 12
prioritizing, 7–8, 14, 45–46, 55, 61
problem-solving, 35–36, 41, 63–64, 87
process, 27–30, 69–71, 99
process instructions, 33–34
process loss, 99
production process, 69–71

Q TIP, 53
Questions, debriefing and, 107-109
Quick Vote, 55

Rainbow Connections, 57–58
rank order vote, 55
Read All About It!, 59–60
recall, 39
reconnecting, 75
Red Dot, Blue Dot, 61–62
relevance, vii
roles, 15, 37, 48
Round Robin method, 10

SAGE process, 108
Save Everybody!, 63–64
Scolton, Beth, 94
self-policing, 46
Self-selection method, 12
sharing phase, 108
silence, 108
silent sorting, 6
simplicity, 10, vii
size of group. *see* team size
Slip method, 10
Soda Can Carry, 65–66
Sound of Music, The, 67–68
Stop Whining – and Start Winning!, 68
Stratified method, 12
straw poll, 83–84
Streamline the Process, 69–71
streamlining, 69–71
Stretch Goals, 73
sub-teams, 11–12

Task roles, 15
team building, 43
Team Openers, 81–82
Team Process Puzzle, 77–79
team size
    3, groups of, 77, 105
    3-5, groups of, 25
    3-6, groups of, 91
    4 groups of equal size, 103
    4-8, groups of, 65, 87
    4-10, groups of, 89
    5+, groups of, 97, 99
    5-6, groups of, 3, 39
    5-15, groups of, 35, 45
    5-20, groups of, 49

5-25, groups of, 51
5-30, groups of, 43
6+, groups of, 37, 47, 63
6-10, groups of, 17
6-24, groups of, 57
8+, groups of, 93
8-10, groups of, 95
8-16, groups of, 85
8-20, groups of, 1
10-20, groups of, 69
10-30, groups of, 5
12-20, groups of, 27
any size, 7, 9, 11, 13, 15, 19, 21, 23, 31, 33, 41, 53, 55, 61, 67, 73, 75, 81, 83, 101
teamwork, value of, 47, 89–90, 91–92, 105–106
Tea Time, 75
Test for Consensus, 83–84
Thiagi, 107
Thompson, Linda, 53
time, debriefing and, 107
time limits, 41, vii
time management, 7–8
time required
1-3 minutes, 11
2 minutes of explanation, 23
5 minutes, 33, 53, 101
5-10 minutes, 9, 13, 21, 73, 81
5-15 minutes, 41, 67, 75
5-20 minutes, 49, 51
10 minutes, 7, 19, 55, 61, 83, 93, 105
10-15 minutes, 1, 17, 35, 47, 61, 87, 95
10-20 minutes, 97
15 minutes, 57, 99
15-20 minutes, 3, 5, 39, 43, 45, 103
20 minutes, 25, 63, 77
20-25 minutes, 91
20-30 minutes, 15, 69
30 minutes, 27, 39, 65, 85, 89
60 minutes set up, 31
Tinker Toys, 85
Titanic, 63
To Build a Bridge, 87–88
To Build a Tower, 89–90
To Build a Tower, Version Two, 91–92
transfer phase, 109
treatment of others, 95
Tug of War, 93–94

Virtual teams, 31
vision, collective, 101
vision statements, 60
Visualization method, 10
Vive La Difference method, 10
Volunteers method, 11
voting, 55

Walking Our Talk, 95
wallflowers, vii
warm-ups, vii
Web We Weave, The, 97–98
Weisman, Carol, 95
"what" questions, 108
When Shall We Meet Again?, 99–100
"when" questions, 109
Where Are We Going?, 101–102
"why" questions, 108
Win or Lose?, 103–104
Woody, Neicy, 75

You're The Expert!, 105–106

Contributors

Mr. Jeff Anthony
113 Willards Way
Yorktown, VA 23693-2544
Phone (757) 766-3132
Fax (757) 766-3132
email silverspur@cox.net

Dr. Marlene Caroselli
Center for Professional Development
324 Latona Road
Rochester, NY 14626
Phone (716)227-6512
Fax (509)696-5405
email mccpd@aol.com
http://hometown.aol.com/mccpd

Ms. Chris Clarke-Epstein, CSP
SPEAKING!
P.O. Box 37
Wausau, WI 54402-0037
Phone (715)842-2467
Fax (715)848-9463
email Chris@ChrisClarke-Epstein.com
http://www.ChrisClarke-Epstein.com

Ms. Ellen Domb, Ph.D.
PQR Group
190 N. Mountain Avenue
Upland, CA 91786
Phone (909)949-0857
Fax (909)949-2986
email ellendomb@compuserve.com
http://www.triz-journal.com

Ms. Kay Friedinger
Director, Center for Performance
Excellence
Missouri Department of Revenue
P.O. Box 325
Jefferson City, MO 65105-0325
Phone (573) 751-0225
Fax (573)526-2019
email kay_freidinger@mail.dor.state.mo.us

Merri Hanson
Peninsula Mediation Center
217 McLaws Circle, Suite 1
Williamsburg, VA 23185
Phone (757) 253-7677
Fax (757)253-7688
email office@peninsulamediation.com
http://www.peninsulamediation.com

Gail Howerton, MA, CLP, CLL
CEO (Chief Energizing Officer),
Funcilitators
1236 Breckenridge Circle
Riva, MD 21140
Phone (800)930-6096
Fax(410)956-3231
email gail@funcilitators.com
http://www.funcilitators.com

Brother Richard Dube, CFA
Alexian Brothers Sherbrooke Village
4005 Ripa Avenue
St. Louis, MO 63125
Phone (314)544-1111
Fax (314)544-5134
email brodube@aol.com

Beth Scolton
Caterpillar Inc.
100 N.E. Adams Street
Peoria, IL 61629

Linda Thompson
Staff Development Instructor
Henrico County Public Schools
Box 23120
Richmond, VA 23223
Phone (804)652-3679
Fax (804)652-3872
email lkthomps@henrico.k12.va.us
http://wwww.henrico.k12.va.us

Carol Weisman, CSP
Board Builders
48 Granada Way
St. Louis, MO 63124
Phone (888)500-1777
Fax (314)991-3018
email cewfer@aol.com
http://www.carolweisman.com

Kristin J. Arnold, CMC, CPF, CSP helps corporations, government and non-profit organizations achieve extraordinary results. With years of team-building and facilitation experience, Kristin specializes in coaching executives and their leadership, management and employee teams to be *extraordinary*.

In addition to facilitation services, QPC Inc. offers diversified programs around the team concept to meet the needs of CEOs, COOs, executives, managers and team members. Her highly customized speeches and seminars have become instrumental in achieving higher performance and exceptional results within the workplace.

An accomplished author and editor of several books, professional articles and audiocassette tapes, as well as a featured columnist in *The Daily Press*, Kristin is regarded as an expert in team development, facilitation and process improvement techniques.

For more information on how Kristin can help your teams become extraordinary, contact her at:

Quality Process Consultants, Inc.
11304 Megan Drive
Fairfax, Virginia 22030
(703) 278.0892 or 800.589.4733
www.qpcteam.com

Order Form

Postal orders: QPC Press, 11304 Megan Drive, Fairfax, VA 22030

Phone orders: (800) 589.4733 or (703) 278.0892

Fax orders: (703) 278.0891

Internet orders: www.qpcteam.com

Please send me the following books:

___ *Team Energizers: Fifty Practical Team Activities*		$19.95
___ *Team Basics: Practical Strategies for Team Success*		$14.95
___ *Email Basics: Practical Tips to Improve Team Communication*		$ 6.95
___ *Team Openers: 100 Questions to Warm-Up Your Team*		$ 6.95

Please send me the following audio products:

___ *Facilitation Skills Audiocassette Series*		$49.99
___ *The Extraordinary Team Music CD*		$ 7.95

Subtotal   _____

Sales Tax: Add 4.5% for products shipped to Virginia addresses   _____

U.S. Shipping: Add $4 for first product   _____
                 Add $2 for each additional product

Total   _____

Payment: ☐ Check   ☐ Credit Card: Visa   MasterCard   AMEX

Card number:_____ Exp. Date:____/_____

Name:_____

Company:_____Email:_____

Address:_____

Phone:_____Fax:_____

Signature:_____

Rule A:
Don't Adjust — Aim at the Target

Rule B:
Correct −z from Last Aiming

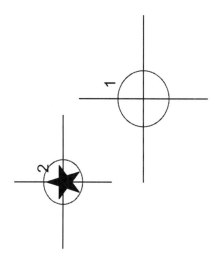

Rule C:
Correct −z from Target

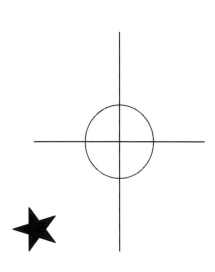

Rule D:
Aim at Last Landing Position

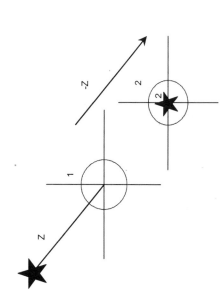

Key

 Target

★ Landing Position

 Distance z measured from target to landing position

 Distance z measured from target in opposite direction (180°)

Key

 Target

★ Landing Position

Distance z measured from target to landing position

Distance z measured from target in opposite direction (180°)

Key

 Target

★ Landing Position

 Distance z measured from target to landing position

Distance z measured from target in opposite direction (180°)

Key

Target

★ Landing Position

 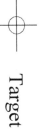 Distance z measured from target to landing position

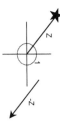 Distance z measured from target in opposite direction (180°)

ML

S/04